stitch it: home

21 craft projects to make for your home

inspirations books

contents

living

dining

bed & bath

just for you

tools & techniques

living

lampshade deluxe

The iridescent glass beads and brass pendants catch the light and scatter it in a shimmering show.

The design of this beaded mesh was inspired by the coffin cover of an Egyptian mummy: the teenage daughter of a wealthy family had her sarcophagus adorned with a beaded design similar to this. It's amazing to think that the techniques of both bead-making and beadwork have remained largely unchanged over such a long period of time.

Bugle beads in Egyptian times were made by rolling faience, a clay material, around a string. When the clay was baked, the string burned away and left a hollow in the centre of the bead. The minerals in the clay determined the final colour of the beads. These days bugle beads are made from a drawn tube of glass that is simply cut into segments of the desired length.

materials and techniques

This project uses four types of beads, all of which are commonly available: seed beads and bugle beads, Czech cut-crystal beads and brass beads. The seed beads and bugle beads are finished with an aurora borealis coating. This finish, also called rainbow, AB or iris in bead catalogues, adds a rainbow appearance to the base colour, almost like a film of oil on water. Many bead sizes are measured in millimetres, although seed beads have a numbering system in which a larger number represents a smaller bead. This is because the system is based on the number of beads that fit into a standard unit of measurement.

A plain lampshade gets a touch of glamour with a skirt of aurora borealis beads, with heart-shaped brass droplets adding romantic highlights.

lampshade deluxe

materials

Plain fabric or cardboard lampshade,
approximately 4in (10cm) diameter at top
edge and 6¼in (16cm) high
4oz (100g) of 11/0 seed beads
10oz (300g) of 7mm long bugle beads
120 4mm faceted Bohemian crystal beads
60 4mm round brass Bali beads
60 small heart-shaped brass Bali beads
Beading thread to match lampshade
Big-eye beading needle or no. 10 beading needle
Sewing needle (optional: see step one)
Basic sewing equipment (see page 122)

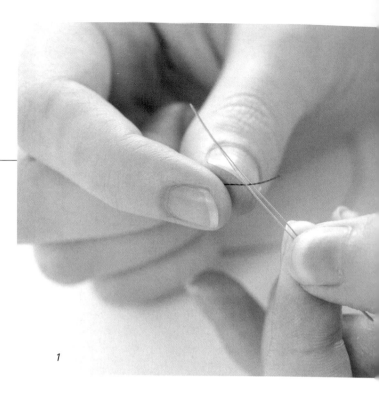

1

step one

The beading needle used for this project is sold as "The
Big Eye" needle in many haberdashery and beading
supply stores. It is fine enough to pass through small
seed beads and it is easy to thread because the needle
splits down the centre to accept the thread, then
springs back together to hold it in place.

If your beading needle is not strong enough to go
through the fabric of the lampshade, you will need to
use a sewing needle. Some fine sewing needles will
pass through the holes of seed beads. Otherwise, you
will need to unthread the sewing needle and insert the
thread into the beading needle to allow you to thread
on the bead, then unthread the beading needle and
reinsert the thread into the sewing needle to stitch
through the shade again.

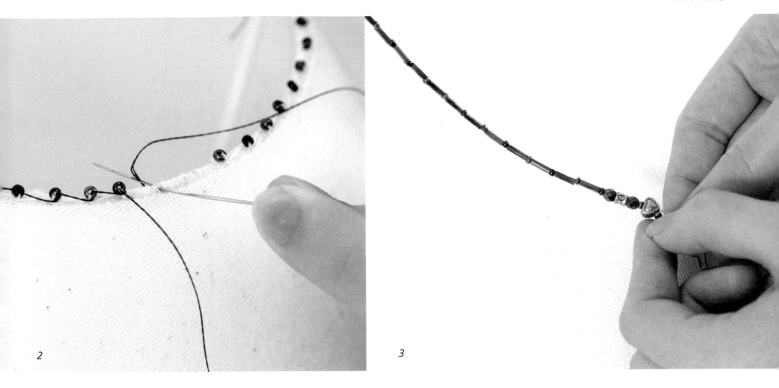

2

3

step two

Begin by stitching seed beads around the top of the lampshade, spacing them at approximately ¼in (6mm) intervals. We have used black thread in the photographs on these pages to make the stitching visible against the pale shade.

Bring the beading thread up to the top of the shade from underneath the top rim, add a seed bead and then stitch through the top edge of the lampshade. Take the thread across to the position of the next bead, then stitch through the rim again. Add the next bead and stitch through the rim again before moving on to the next position.

step three

Working with a length of beading thread about one yard (one metre) long, pass the needle and thread through the first seed bead on the rim of the lampshade. Thread the first row of beads onto the thread, alternating bugle beads and seed beads. Continue until three or four bugle beads hang below the lower edge of the lampshade. The extra beads are required because the honeycomb pattern makes the mesh shorten as it's stretched out.

After the last seed bead in the row, add a faceted Bohemian crystal bead, a round brass Bali bead, another faceted bead and then another seed bead. Lastly add a brass heart and another seed bead. The last seed bead will act as an anchor as you work back up the strand to create the mesh. Refer to the diagram on page 11 for details.

lampshade deluxe

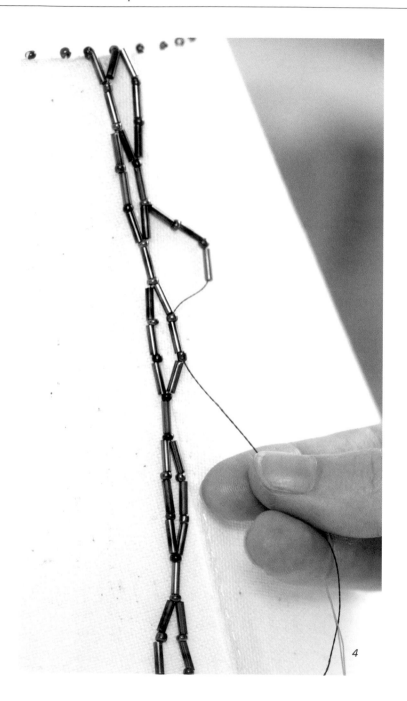

4

step four

Take the beading needle and thread and pass them back through the brass heart and all the beads of the drop section, up to the first bugle bead and the seed bead above it. At this stage you start to create the honeycomb mesh. Add a bugle bead, a seed bead, a bugle bead, a seed bead, and a third bugle bead. Skip the same number of beads on the original row and slide the beading needle and thread through the next seed bead, bugle bead and seed bead. Refer to the diagram opposite for details.

Repeat this until you reach the top of the row. Pass the beading thread through the next seed bead on the rim of the shade and anchor the row by stitching through the fabric. (Change to the sewing needle again if necessary.)

Bring the needle to the front through the same seed bead. Now work back downwards to create the next row. Add three new bugle beads alternating with seed beads and pass the needle and thread through the center section of the honeycomb on the previous row. Refer to the diagram opposite for details.

step five

As you stitch, keep an eye on the remaining length of beading thread. You always need to finish off the thread at the rim of the lampshade where you can anchor it and knot the end before starting a new thread. Before starting a new row of beads at the rim of the shade, check that you have at least enough thread remaining to work the next two rows, down and up. If not, fasten off the thread with a secure knot inside the lampshade and start with a new length of beading thread.

Continue working around the lampshade until you reach the last seed bead at the top. Work down to the bottom, turn around and work back through the heart and all the beads of the drop section as before. To link the honeycombs together, instead of adding three new bugle beads and alternate seed beads for each loop, add just one bugle bead, then pass the needle and thread through the center section of the honeycomb of the first row. Add another bugle bead and pass the needle through the corresponding beads of the previous row, and so on until you reach the top. Refer to the diagram for details.

When you reach the top, pass the beading needle and thread through the first seed bead, then stitch through the rim of the lampshade. Fasten off the beading thread with a secure knot inside the lampshade.

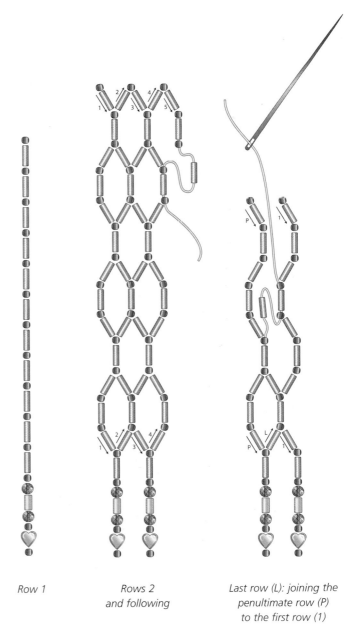

Row 1

Rows 2
and following

Last row (L): joining the
penultimate row (P)
to the first row (1)

at your feet

Wool embroidered flowers add softness to the sturdy burlap of this welcome mat.

Pretty pansies are a garden favourite, and the range of color means that you can embroider them in various shades to suit the décor of your home. The soft pinks and purples of this posy are complemented by a fabric border in deep aubergine. Forget-me-nots help fill the spaces between the flowers and leaves. The last few stitches of embroidery are worked after the border and backing is applied so that they will overlap.

materials and techniques

Burlap is a great material for wool embroidery, as the needle and yarn pass easily through the open weave of the fabric. The woollen yarn lends itself to the soft textures created by long-and-short stitch, which also allow the different colors to blend together without a harsh edge.

The burlap by itself will not provide a stable floor mat, so add a non-slip rubber backing for security. Finish the completed mat with a fabric protector spray that will repel dirt, moisture and stains.

Put out the welcome mat for friends and family and bring a corner of the garden inside.

at your feet

materials

Two pieces of burlap, each 16in x 20in
(40cm x 50cm)

16in x 20in (40cm x 50cm) rubber non-slip
backing

16in (40cm) medium-weight furnishing fabric
(such as blockout-coated curtain fabric)

Machine sewing thread to match furnishing fabric

One skein each of DMC Tapestry Wool in dark
antique violet (7266), medium antique violet
(7262), light antique violet (7120), light pale
yellow (7745), baby blue (7322), moss green
(7362), light moss green (7361)

Tapestry needle, no. 20

Chenille needle, no. 20 (optional)

Tailor's chalk

Spray-on fabric protector

Basic sewing equipment (see page 122)

step one

Machine stitch ¾in (2cm) inside the perimeter of one piece of the burlap to mark the seam allowance and stabilize the fabric. Use a long machine basting stitch. Using this stitching line as a guide, enlarge and trace or copy the embroidery design from page 138 onto a corner of the burlap, using tailor's chalk. You only need to transfer the basic outlines of the design, then simply refer to the diagram as you add the details.

The embroidery stitches used for this project are all shown in detail on pages 129–37.

2

3

step two

Begin the embroidery with the center of the largest
pansy. With the dark antique violet (7266) thread,
make a triangle of three straight stitches to mark
the angles of the petals. (These stitches will later be
covered by French knots.) Work long stitches radiating
out from the center of the flower. Work around the
center from left to right, leaving a one-stitch gap
between each long stitch. Vary the length of the
stitches a little.

Once you have worked around the three petals,
work back from right to left, making shorter stitches
between the long ones. If any large gaps remain, fill
them with long or short stitches as necessary. This
method of working long-and-short stitch is a little
different from the usual method.

step three

Change to the medium antique violet (7262) thread.
Beginning at the left-hand edge of the petals, work
a long stitch at the end of each darker stitch. When
you reach the right-hand edge, work back from right
to left, filling in the gaps between the stitches with
shorter stitches.

Complete the petals by filling in the remaining area
out to the outline with long-and-short stitches.
The fourth petal is worked in a single color, using
long-and-short stitch in the traditional way (see
page 134) to fill in the shape.

Choose a contrasting color (such as light pale yellow,
7745) and work three or four French knots (three
wraps) at the center of the flower, then three straight
stitches radiating from the center out onto the petals.

4

step four

Complete the smaller pansies in the same manner as the larger, following the colors indicated in the photograph at left. The leaves are also worked in long-and-short stitch using light moss green (7361); wait until after the mat is assembled to complete these so that they overlap the fabric border.

Work the forget-me-nots with light pale yellow (7745) centers and baby blue (7322) petals. Make the French knots for both the center and the petals by wrapping the yarn around the needle three times and stitching over one thread of the burlap.

Finally, fill in the areas between the flowers and leaves with a random scattering of short running stitches in moss green (7362) yarn.

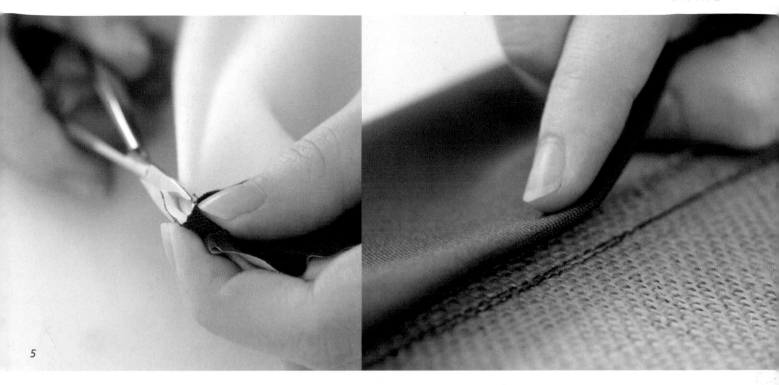

5

step five

Layer the embroidered burlap with the remaining piece
and the rubber non-slip backing and stitch the layers
together around the seam allowance. Cut border pieces
from the furnishing fabric, by enlarging and using the
patterns on page 138. Cut two of each piece. Place one
long strip and one short strip with right sides together
and the points aligned at one end. Stitch up and down
the diagonal sides, leaving ½in (12mm) unstitched at
each end. Trim the fabric at the point, close to the
stitching. Repeat with the remaining two pieces of
border fabric, giving two "L" shapes. Now join the long
piece of one "L" to the short piece of the other "L"
in the same way, and then repeat with the remaining
corner to create a rectangular border.

Turn the border right-side out and press under ½in
(12mm) on both front and back inside edges.

step six

With the right side of the border facing the wrong side
of the mat, stitch the inner edge of the border along the
pressed line to the seam allowance of the mat. Turn the
border over the edges of the mat. Pin and hand stitch the
hem of the border to the front of the mat, ensuring that
it sits straight on the grain of the burlap. Finish the border
with a line of machine top-stitching just inside the edge
of the fabric.

Work the remaining embroidery over the edge of the border.
Pass the needle between the layers of your mat so that
the stitching doesn't show on the back. It may take a little
wiggling to get the tapestry needle through the border
fabric, but you can try making a small hole with a pin or to
get each stitch started, or switch to a chenille needle.

Spray the mat with a fabric protector such as Scotchguard™
to prevent stains and water damage.

magnificent magnolias

Bring a touch of spring indoors with this elegant cross-stitched design.

The large, dish-like flowers of the magnolia bloom in the spring; they are a harbinger of the season to come as the flowers show before the earliest leaves on this deciduous tree. Despite their generous size, the petals are quite delicate and easily bruised. They can be used as cut flowers for interior decoration but the season for picking them is short.

If you love magnolia flowers, you can enjoy them in your home all year round. This cross-stitch design is simple to create and can be used on a cushion, with parts of the design repeated on other furnishings such as a linen sofa throw or a coffee-table runner to tie your décor together.

materials and techniques

The colours of delicate blue-and-white porcelain are used in the cushion shown on these pages, against a background of natural linen. Your choice of colours can be dictated by the décor of your living room by simply replacing the shades of blue with similar shades of a different colour. Shades of magenta to soft lilac used with the white would add a more realistic colour scheme, while green tones would give a fresh, spring-like feel to the design. You can also change the colour of the background fabric for a different look: stitching on a dark-coloured linen will make the design stand out in contrast, while a white or pale background will give a more subtle overall effect.

The matching sofa throw is created in linen the same colour as one of the embroidery threads and trimmed with the same piping as the cushion. You could embroider a small section of the design onto a corner of the throw.

magnificent magnolias

1

materials

14in (36cm) square of natural evenweave linen,
    28 count

1 skein each of DMC stranded cotton in light
    grey blue (159), medium grey blue (160), grey
    blue (161), dark navy blue (823) and winter
    white (3865)

14in (36cm) square of dark blue velvet or faux
    suede fabric

Matching dark blue machine sewing thread

60in (1.5m) dark blue thick cord

14in (35cm) cushion insert

Tapestry needle, no. 26

Basic sewing equipment (see page 122)

step one

Find the center of the linen square by folding it in half
each way, pressing a crease with your fingers. This will
help you center your design. You may find it helpful to
work a line of tacking along each of the folded center
lines, to guide your stitching.

Neaten the edges of the linen square by overlocking
or blanket stitching to prevent fraying while you are
working the embroidery.

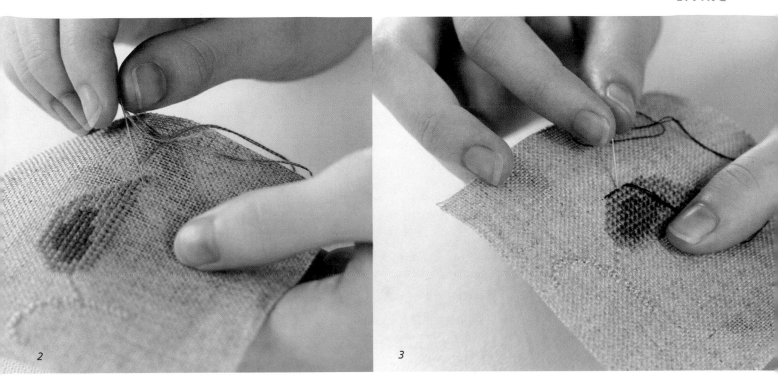

2

3

step two

Working from the center of the design, stitch each
cross stitch over two threads following the chart on
page 139 for colour and placement. Use two strands
of embroidery thread. To begin stitching, hold a small
tail of thread at the back of the fabric and work the
first six or seven stitches so that the tail is trapped
underneath them. Finish each length of thread by
passing the needle under six or seven stitches on the
back of the work to secure the thread. Trim off the tail
of thread close to the stitching. Ensure that you work
all of the cross stitches with the diagonals lying in the
same direction. To do this, work the first diagonals of
all the crosses in a row from left to right, then work
back along the row completing all of the crosses
with the opposite diagonal. See page 131 for more
information on working cross stitch.

step three

When all the cross stitching is complete, stitch around
the outside of the design in back stitch, using two
strands of the darkest shade of thread. Remove the
tacking stitches and press the design gently from the
back using a steam iron and pressing cloth.
Place the embroidered linen and the dark blue fabric
with right sides together. Machine stitch around all sides,
using a 5/8in (1.5cm) seam allowance, and leaving an
8in (20cm) opening at the center of the lower edge. Turn
to the right side. Place the cushion insert inside. Using
a small ladder stitch, sew the opening almost closed,
leaving an opening of 1in (2.5cm) in the middle.
Lay the dark blue cord around the edges of the cushion,
tucking the ends into the opening. Use slip stitch to
secure the cord in place around the seam of the cushion
and stitch the opening closed.

rust & recreation

A casual throw for keeping off a cool breeze takes on unique hues when dyed using rusted metal.

Rust is the name given to the orange, powdery coating that forms on iron objects when they are exposed to moisture, either from the air or water. It is formed by oxidation, a chemical reaction between the iron and oxygen. Rust is normally considered undesirable, because metal that is rusted is weaker than uncorroded metal. The bright orange or dull reddish brown color, though, often gives a beautiful finish to old ironware such as jardinière pots, or to weathered wooden fences with rusty nails. Antique metal implements that are no longer used for their original purpose, such as horseshoes and old machine cogs, can be decorative objects in their own right with a gorgeous patina of age in their rusty surfaces.

materials and techniques

Dyeing fabric with rust is simple and effective. The easiest and safest method to colour fabric with rust is to collect rusted objects such as chains, nails, old tools, horseshoes, tin cans, and so on. This piece of fabric was dyed using a length of rusty chain, giving a mottled effect, but you can achieve a multitude of patterns using other objects, alone or all together.

Creating your own fabrics can be very rewarding and add a personal touch to your home.

rust & recreation

1

materials

50in x 72in (130cm x 180cm) natural fibre fabric
such as silk, cotton or linen
Rusted objects such as chains, horseshoes, old
tools and tins, nails and bolts
Plastic work sheet, such as a painter's drop sheet
Water
1 cup white vinegar in a spray bottle
1 cup kitchen salt
String (optional: see step two)
Large plastic bag that seals securely
7yd (6.5m) braid, fringe or ribbon for the border
Washing detergent and fabric softener
Basic sewing equipment (see page 122)

step one

Spread a plastic drop sheet over your working area.
Soak the fabric in water and squeeze out the excess.
Spray the fabric generously with white vinegar.
Alternatively, you can soak the fabric in a solution of
vinegar to begin with. (Depending on the size of your
piece of fabric, you can soak it in pure vinegar or add
up to four cups of water to every cup of vinegar.)
Lay out the vinegar-soaked fabric onto the plastic sheet
and place the rusted objects on the fabric. You can
place them randomly or deliberately create a pattern.
Sprinkle kitchen salt over the rusted pieces and then
respray with vinegar – be generous with the amount
of salt and vinegar.

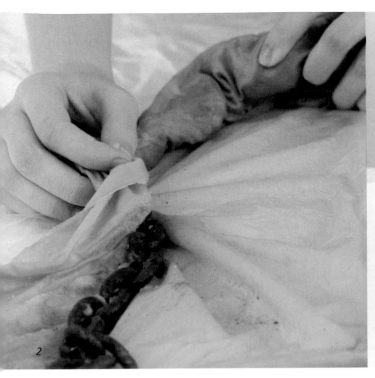

step two

Fold or roll up the fabric with the rusty objects inside. If you want a lot of rust coloring, make sure as much of the fabric as possible is near the rusted objects. If you are using silk, make sure you don't snag the silk on the metal. You may need to tie the fabric together with string if the fabric is not making enough contact with the rusted objects.

Place the piece in a large plastic bag and seal it up. Leave it in a warm, sunny spot (this speeds up the process). Protect the area from any possible leaks. Leave the piece for three to six days (depending on how much rust color you want the fabric to take and how quickly the color transfer is occurring). You can unwrap and reposition the rusted objects, apply more salt and vinegar and roll the fabric up again for another few days if you want to color other areas and overlap color.

step three

After three to six days, take the fabric out of the plastic bag, unroll the fabric and remove the rusted objects. Store them for future use if you wish; however, they can be reused immediately (you don't need to wait for more rust to develop). Rinse away the salt and vinegar.

Wash the fabric in a washing machine for cotton and linen or by hand if using silk. Use your preferred washing detergent and fabric softener. Let the fabric air dry on the clothesline or an indoor drying rack. Finish the edges of the fabric by turning a narrow hem and sewing on a braid, fringe or ribbon.

soft touch

Turn an address book or photograph album into a personal treasure.

Diaries, address books, notebooks and photograph albums are essential for organising your life and your memories. Adding a beautiful embroidered fabric cover turns these necessities into something special. With their pretty butterflies, beads and flowers, they can be left on display so the details they contain are close at hand when required.

materials and techniques

The butterfly and appliqué flower are created using double-sided fusible interfacing (also known as appliqué paper), so you don't have to worry about finishing the edges. Instead, metallic embroidery threads are used to work back stitch around the outline of the flower and help it to stand out from the background fabric. The double-sided butterfly is gathered slightly down the body line and stitched down only in the center to give it a three-dimensional finish, as though it is ready to fly away any second!

Keep your essential addresses and memorable photographs close at hand: you won't want to hide these books in a drawer.

soft touch

materials

20in (50cm) silk shantung

20in (50cm) thin polyester batting

4in (10cm) square of double-sided fusible interfacing

Forty 3mm pearl beads

Two 15/0 gold seed beads

1 skein of silk pearl embroidery thread to match the fabric

1 skein of Madeira Metallic no. 40, gold-8 embroidery thread

Crewel needles, no. 7 and no. 10

Fine betweens needle, no. 9, or beading needle, no. 10

2B pencil, water-soluble fabric marker or tailor's chalk

Thin card or template plastic

Basic sewing equipment (see page 122)

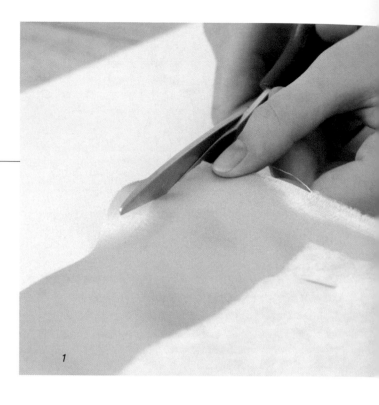

1

step one

Fold the thin polyester batting around the outside cover of the book, front and back. Using all-purpose scissors, carefully trim the batting to the same size as the book cover. You can now use the batting as a template when cutting the fabric for the cover: lay the batting on the wrong side of the fabric, leaving an allowance of at least 1in (2.5cm) at the top and bottom edges, and 4in (10cm) on either side edge of the batting. Baste the batting to the fabric using sewing cotton and long stitches. Baste along the side of the spine to mark where the front cover begins.

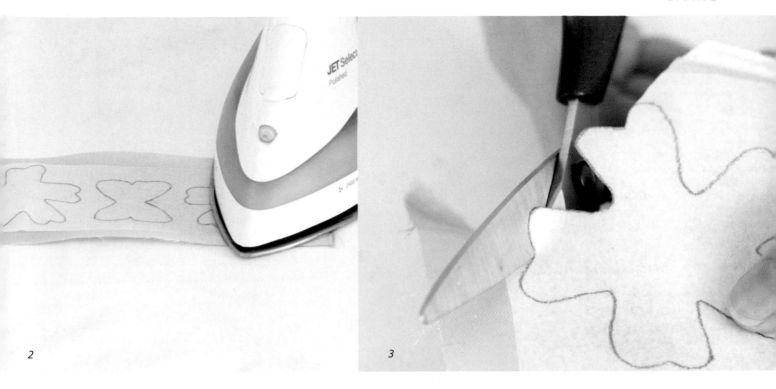

2

3

step two

Trace the flower and butterfly shapes from page 140
onto the paper side of the double-sided fusible
interfacing and cut around them roughly. Trace the
flower shape onto thin card or template plastic and
cut out a template. Mark one side of the template as
the right side, although you will use both sides to give
some variation to the flower shapes.

Following the manufacturer's instructions, iron the
double-sided fusible interfacing onto the wrong side
of a scrap of the silk fabric. Cut out the butterfly
shape on the line and remove the backing paper. Lay
the butterfly shape with the fusible side down on
the wrong side of another scrap of the fabric. Again
following the manufacturer's instructions, iron the
butterfly shape onto the fabric. Carefully cut the wings
out around the first shape. Set aside.

step three

Cut out the flower shape on the line and remove
the backing paper. Place the flower with the fusible
side down in the center of the lower half of the
front cover. Try to turn the flower so the grain of the
fabric is at an angle to the grain of the cover. Again
following the manufacturer's instructions, iron the
flower onto the fabric.

Lay the flower template on top of the flower so that
it partly overlaps and trace around the shape using
a sharp pencil, water-soluble marking pen or tailor's
chalk. Do not trace the part of the shape that overlaps
the appliqué flower. Turn the flower template over and
reposition it so that it overlaps a different part of the
flower, tracing it as before. Repeat, so that you have
two or three overlapping traced flower shapes.

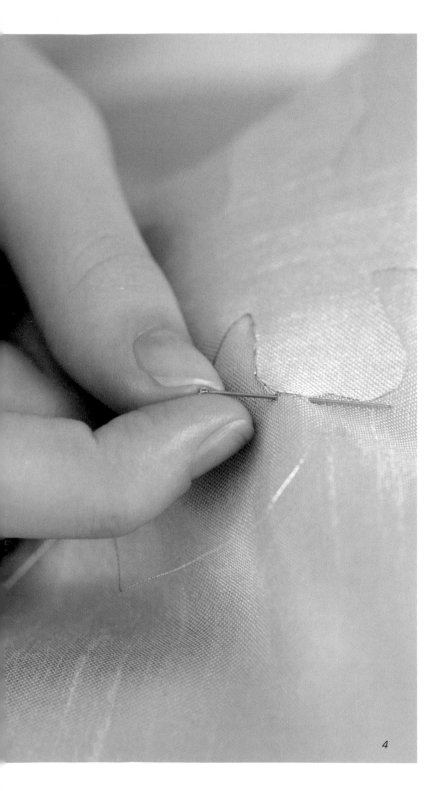

step four

Using one strand of silk embroidery thread and a no. 7 crewel needle, stitch the outline of the first flower in running stitch. Repeat for the second flower shape, using outline stitch. Work the third flower in whipped running stitch. For information about working the stitches used in this project, see pages 129–37.

Using one strand of gold metallic embroidery thread and a no. 10 crewel needle, stitch around the outside of the appliqué flower in back stitch. Use the gold thread and running stitch to stitch a smaller flower shape inside the appliqué one.

Still using the gold embroidery thread, make a line of small running stitches down the center of the butterfly shape, pulling them tight to slightly gather the shape. Make two small back stitches to anchor the thread and hold the gathering in place. Position the butterfly on the front cover of the book and use the gold embroidery thread to stitch it down with two or three long straight stitches down the center. Finish the body by working padded satin stitch across the straight stitches.

Finally, make two straight stitches for the antennae, adding a tiny gold bead at the tip of each stitch.

4

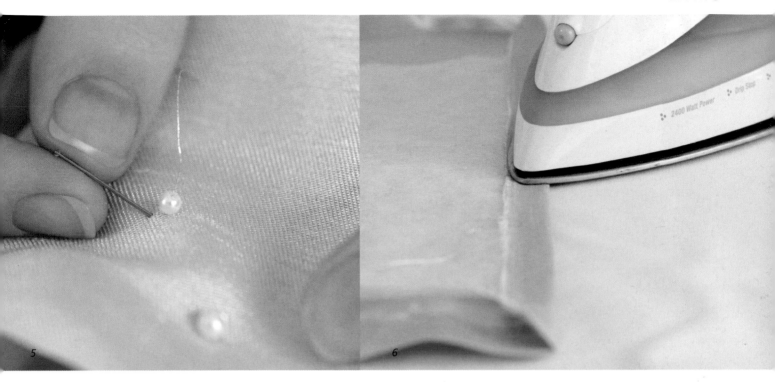

5

6

step five

Begin adding pearl beads in offset rows: that is, place the top row of beads 2in (5cm) apart, then place the second row ¾in (2cm) below the first, with the beads aligned with the center of the spaces in the first row. Mark the positions of the beads with a temporary fabric marker or basting stitches before you start stitching. Use the gold embroidery thread and the betweens needle to attach the pearls. If the betweens needle won't pass through the holes in the beads, use a beading needle instead.

Once the embroidery is completed, remove any markings (tailor's chalk, water-soluble marker or pencil) using the manufacturer's recommended method.

step six

Use an iron to press under a 5cm (2in) hem on each of the side edges of the fabric, then use the iron to carefully press the upper and lower hem allowances over the batting. Be careful not to allow the iron to touch the exposed batting or the pearl beads. Now press the side flaps over the batting.

Align the book on the batting and fold the flaps over the edges of the covers. Pin the flaps to the fabric of the front and back covers at the upper and lower corners of the book. With the book closed, use ladder stitch to stitch the flaps to the outside cover fabric, creating pockets for the book covers to sit in. Remove any basting stitches.

ornaments d'or

Dress up your Christmas tree with these beautifully embroidered and beaded decorations.

A pretty handstitched ornament adds a unique touch to your festive décor. These decorations would make precious gifts for your family and friends. Simply stitch names and dates onto the fabric for the back of the ornament. They will become treasured keepsakes.

materials and techniques

Metallic embroidery thread gives rich overtones to the embellishment on these ornaments. Stitching with metallic threads is a little different to stitching with cotton, silk or rayon. The threads can tend to fray or break, so work with short lengths – fingertip to elbow is ideal. Make sure that the needle you choose is a suitable size: it should make a large enough hole in the fabric to allow the thread to pass easily through, without being too big.

Whatever your decorating style, these delicate ornaments will be dazzling accessories.

ornaments d'or

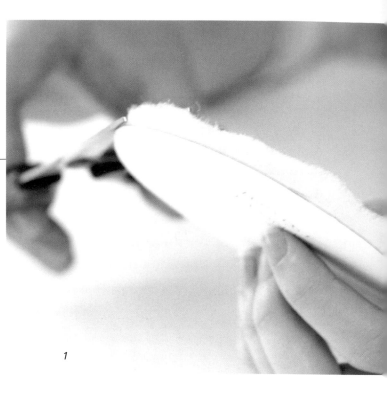

1

materials

*Two 8in (20cm) squares of silk fabric for
    each ornament*
8in (20cm) squares of muslin for each ornament
*DMC metallic embroidery thread in light
    gold (284)*
Madeira metallic thread no. 40, gold-4
Anchor Lamé thread, gold (303)
Beading thread, neutral colour
Sewing thread to match silk fabric
Sewing thread, grey and white
Mill Hill petite beads, gold
Mill Hill glass seed beads, bronze
Forty ¼in (6mm) bugle beads, gold
*2yd 26½in (2.5m) x ¹/₁₆in (2mm) gold metal
    beaded chain*
*13¾in (35cm) beaded fringe, 4–5in
    (10–12.5cm) long*
Straw needle, no. 7
Crewel needle, no. 9
Beading needle, no. 15
6in (15cm) embroidery hoop
Water-soluble fabric marker or tailor's chalk
Tracing paper and pencil
Cardboard for making templates
1 sheet white craft card
12in (30cm) lightweight polyester batting
Craft glue
Basic sewing equipment (see page 122)

step one

Trace the shapes of the decorations from pages 140–1
onto tracing paper. Glue the tracing paper onto
cardboard and cut out the shapes to make templates.
Using the templates, trace two of each shape onto
white craft card. Cut out the shapes. Match each
pair, and use a pencil to mark the inner face of each
cardboard shape. The marked sides will be the ones
that are not covered by fabric.

Apply glue to the front of one cardboard shape from
each pair. The front is the unmarked side. Press the card
lightly onto the batting. Trim the batting to the edges
of the card with scissors.

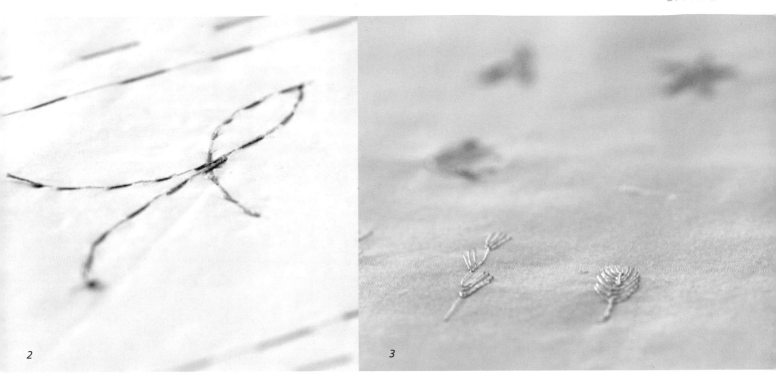

2

3

step two

Using tracing paper, trace the outline of each shape
from page 140–1. Trace the main lines of the
embroidery design as well.

Place a square of silk fabric right-side up on a square
of muslin as a foundation. Place the two layers of
fabric in the embroidery hoop. Pin the traced design
onto the silk fabric. Baste around the traced shape and
along the main lines of the embroidery design. Sew a
line of basting ½in (12mm) outside the traced shape.
Tear the tracing paper away from the basting. Use a
water-soluble fabric marker or tailor's chalk to lightly
mark the placement of flowers and other parts of the
embroidery with dots.

step three

With the fabric still in the embroidery hoop, work the
embroidery stitches and beading. The instructions on
the following pages describe the basic stitching and
beading techniques for each decoration. For more
instructions on how to work the embroidery stitches,
see pages 129–37.

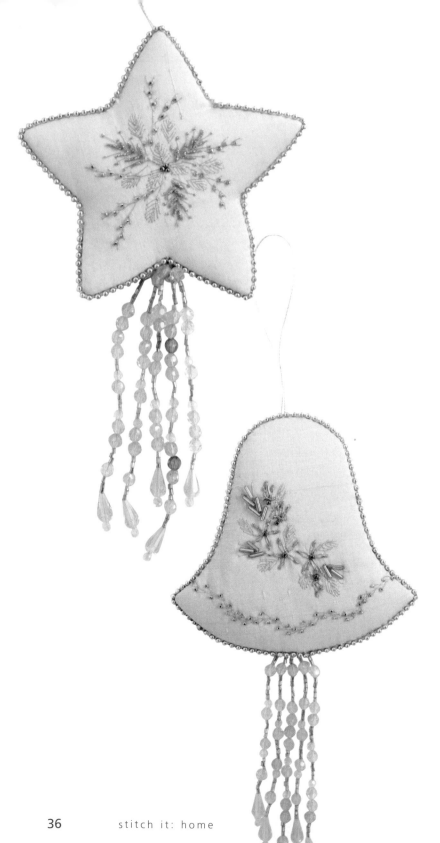

star: Use a single strand of Madeira Metallic gold thread throughout. Work three bullion stitch flower spikes of 20–25 wraps (25 wraps at the bottom of the flower). Work a straight stitch topped by a French knot with three wraps, between the bullions.
Work three feather-stitch leaves in the center. Work feather-stitch sprays and leaves to finish.
Use a beading needle and thread to sew three bronze beads in the center spray of leaves, and sew petite gold beads along the feather-stitch sprays.

bell: Use one strand of Anchor Lamé to work the feather-stitch trim at the lower edge of the bell. Use a beading needle and thread to sew on petite gold beads. Using DMC metallic thread, work three five-petalled flowers and three buds using lazy daisy bullion stitch (four wraps). Work an eight-wrap bullion stitch at the base of each bud with Madeira Metallics gold thread, and sew a bronze bead at the bottom of each bud and in the center of each flower. Use gold bugle beads to make the bead sprays, and work gold straight stitches between the beads. Finish with feather-stitch leaves, using a single strand of the Madeira Metallics gold thread.

stocking: Use a single strand of Madeira Metallics gold thread throughout. Stem stitch the stems. The leaves are lazy daisy stitches. Sew petite gold beads along the ends of the stems with a beading needle and thread. Work straight stitches among the beads.

diamond: Use a single strand of Madeira Metallics gold thread to work the stems in stem stitch, leaves in feather stitch and feather sprays in feather stitch. Use bugle beads, a beading needle and thread to form three floral sprays. Work straight stitches with gold thread between the beads. Attach the petite gold beads to the feather sprays with a beading needle and thread.

triangle: Use Anchor Lamé thread throughout. Stitch the stem-stitch stems and feather-stitch border with one strand of thread. Attach three bugle bead flowers with a beading needle and thread. Work straight stitches with gold thread between the beads, and sew a petite gold bead at the end of the straight stitch. Using two strands of thread, work the feather-stitch sprays. The leaves are lazy daisy bullion stitches (four wraps), using two strands of thread.

heart: Use Madeira Metallics gold thread throughout. Work three bullion stitch daisies, by working ten 30-wrap bullions in a circle. Sew three bronze beads in the centers of the daisies, and sew a petite gold bead at the end of each bullion stitch. Sew stems in stem stitch, using a single strand of gold thread. Embroider buds in groups of three bullions (30 wraps). Fill in the gaps with leaves, using two strands of gold thread.

circle: Use a single strand of Madeira Metallics gold thread to embroider feather stitch around the circular border, and sew on petite gold beads with a beading needle and thread. Embroider three feather-stitch leaves in the center of the floral design using a single strand of Madeira Metallics gold thread. Sew three bronze beads in the center of the leaves, using a beading needle and thread. Use DMC metallic thread to work three lazy daisy bullion stitches (four wraps) for the flowers and three single lazy daisy stitches as buds. Use a single strand of Madeira Metallics gold thread to embroider three straight stitches as stamens and sew a petite gold bead at the end of each straight stitch. Finish by embroidering fern fronds in feather stitch.

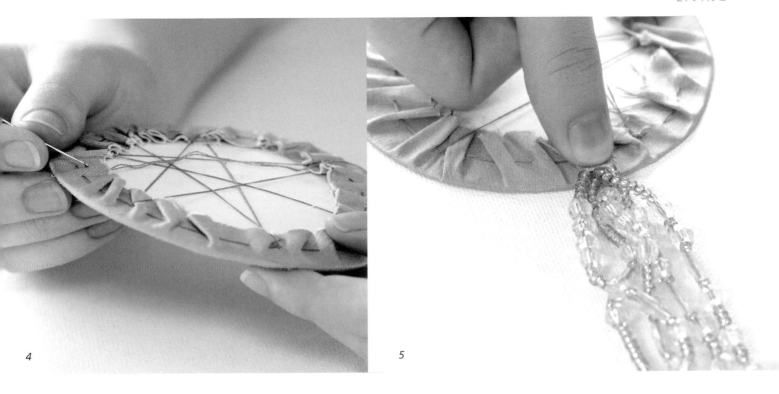

4

5

step four

Cut out the embroidered shape ¾in (2cm) outside the tacked outline. Clip curves where needed before sewing around the seam allowance with a large running stitch for gathering. Position the embroidered fabric over the batting-covered cardboard shape, and gently tighten the gathering thread until the fabric is taut and even on the front. Stitch the edges together across the back of the cardboard as shown in the photograph above, to hold the fabric in place. Cover the outside of the cardboard back with a piece of the same coloured silk.

Cut an 8in (20cm) piece of DMC gold thread, fold it in half and knot the ends to form the hanging loop. Cut a piece of beaded fringe with five strands of beading. Roll up the beaded fringe to make a tassel and place a few stitches through the ribbon at the top to hold it in this shape.

step five

Place a drop of craft glue at the center top and the center bottom of the shape (or at the center top and top corner for the stocking shape). Position the loop of gold thread with the knot in the glue. Position the beaded tassel and press the ribbon down into the craft glue until it sticks well.

Apply craft glue in the center of the cardboard backing, and position the front piece of the decoration on top of the back. Put the decoration aside to dry, placing a heavy book on top to prevent it curling up. When the glue is dry, use thread to match the silk fabric and stitch the two shapes together using slip stitch or ladder stitch. Place the gold beaded chain around the outside of the shape and couch it in place over the join.

dining

festive ribbons

A celebratory swirl of streamers and explosion of embroidered fireworks adorns this simple linen table runner.

A table runner may be used to create a striking feature that runs down the center of the table. A long table runner works best on a rectangular or oval table; if you have a round or square table, you could modify this design by neglecting the repeat and working it on a square mat with tassels at the corners. As well as shortening the runner to suit a round or square table, you could easily lengthen it to suit a refectory-style table, by simply adding another repeat of the design.

materials and techniques

The colors of this design have a festive connotation, employing the traditional red, white and gold of Christmas decorations. Other combinations are also possible: imagine working the streamers in pale greenish-blue and the starbursts in silver. It would also look great with black streamers and pewter starbursts on a grey fabric. Purple streamers and gold stars on a cream background is another option.

Here's a joyful table runner you can use to decorate your table for festive season dinner parties and other special occasions.

festive ribbons

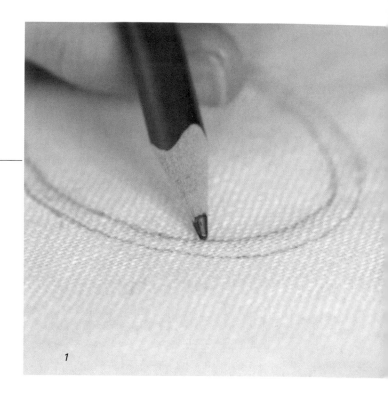

materials

13¾in x 51¼in (35cm x 130cm) off-white
*   linen fabric*
4 skeins Anchor stranded cotton,
*   dark red (44)*
1 skein Anchor Lamé, gold (303)
Crewel needle, no. 5
Water-soluble fabric marker, pencil or
*   tailor's chalk*
Embroidery hoop
Machine sewing thread to match linen
Basic sewing equipment (see page 122)

step one

Wash the fabric before cutting so that it is pre-shrunk.
Enlarge the design on page 142, then trace it onto
one half of the table runner. Turn the pattern around
180 degrees and trace it onto the other half of the
table runner. Use a light box or a sunlit window to
help with the tracing.

Cut the corners from the runner to create the points
at each end as indicated by the pattern. Fold in a ⅜in
(1cm) double hem along all edges. Machine stitch the
hem ¹⁄₁₆in (2mm) from the inside edge.

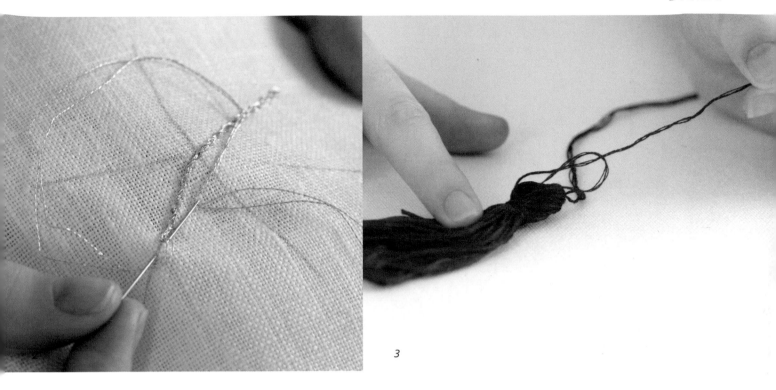

3

step two

Work the streamers in the red embroidery cotton
(using three strands) in padded satin stitch. Stitch just
inside the streamer outlines in chain stitch, then fill in
the wider sections of the streamers with more lines of
chain stitch. Finally, stitch satin stitch across the lines of
chain stitch. See page 135 for instructions on working
this stitch.

Work the starbursts in twisted chain stitch, using
two strands of gold lamé thread. See page 137 for
instructions on working this stitch. Remove any traces
of the fabric marker you used to trace the design
according to the manufacturer's instructions. Allow the
fabric to dry and, while still slightly damp, place the
runner face down on a thick towel and press with a
steam iron.

step three

Make two tassels, using one skein of red stranded cotton for
each. Cut a 12in (30cm) length of thread from each skein
(without unraveling it) and split it into two lengths of three
strands each. Fold the remainder of the skein in half and tie
one of the three-strand lengths around the center of the fold,
leaving the ends long to attach the tassel to the runner. Using
the other three-strand length, lay one end along the tassel and
make a loop at the top of the tassel. Wind rest of this thread
around the tassel about 3/8in (1cm) down from the top, to bind
the tassel and create a cuff. Pass the end of this thread through
the loop, and then pull down on the other end of the thread
(at the bottom of the tassel), until the thread is pulled down
through the cuff to the end of the tassel. Cut all the loops of
thread and trim them to one length. Thread the long ends of
the first three-strand length onto a needle and attach the tassel
to the point at the end of the runner with some strong stitches.

glittering grapes

Bring your own wine in a neat fabric bag tied with whimsical bunches of beaded grapes.

James Boswell called friendship "the wine of life". Conversely, there is little that is more enjoyable than a good bottle of wine shared over a delicious meal with friends. Presented in a practical but decorative bag, your dinner-party gift will be remembered long after the wine is consumed. This project is a great gift idea; however, you may decide to be selfish and keep it for yourself. You could use the weighted cord as a curtain tieback, catching sunlight on the facets of the jeweled grapes and crystal leaves.

materials and techniques

Bottles of wine and champagne make great gifts for many occasions, and the simplicity of this bottle bag means that it is easy to make. A plain cotton fabric is cut in one piece for both outside and lining, eliminating fiddly seams and finishing. You could make several bags at once to stock your gift cupboard.

The fun bunches of bead grapes are also easy to assemble: you simply stitch the beads onto semicircles of felt, then gather the felt around a knot in the end of the cord, adding leaves around the top and vine tendrils of craft wire.

Take a bottle of wine to a dinner party in this beautiful gift bag.

glittering grapes

materials

13¾in x 31½in (35cm x 80cm) plain cotton fabric

Machine sewing thread to match fabric

27½in (70cm) green twisted cord

4in (10cm) square of purple felt

Small amount of polyester fiber fill

1½oz (40g) 7mm faceted purple beads

8–10 small leaf-shaped glass beads (various sizes: minimum length ⅝in or 1.5cm)

Beading thread

Beading needle, no. 10

1 spool 24-gauge green craft wire

Pencil, water-soluble fabric marker or tailor's chalk

Thin card or template plastic

Basic sewing equipment (see page 122)

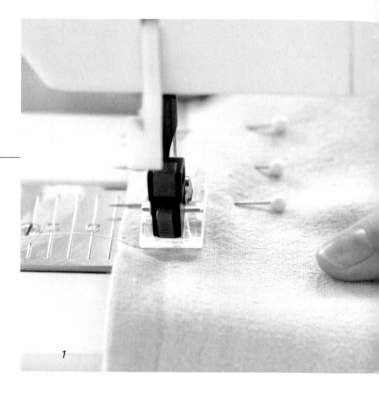

1

step one

Fold the cotton fabric in half with right sides together along the longest axis. This will give you a rectangular shape 31½in (80cm) long and 6⅞in (17.5cm) wide. Pin around all three raw edges. Starting at one short end and using a ⅝in (1.5cm) seam allowance, machine stitch across, then down the long side, stopping 8in (20cm) from the end. Leave a 6in (15cm) opening, then resume stitching to the corner. Turn and stitch across the remaining short side of the rectangle.

Carefully clip the corners off diagonally at all four corners. Press the seams open.

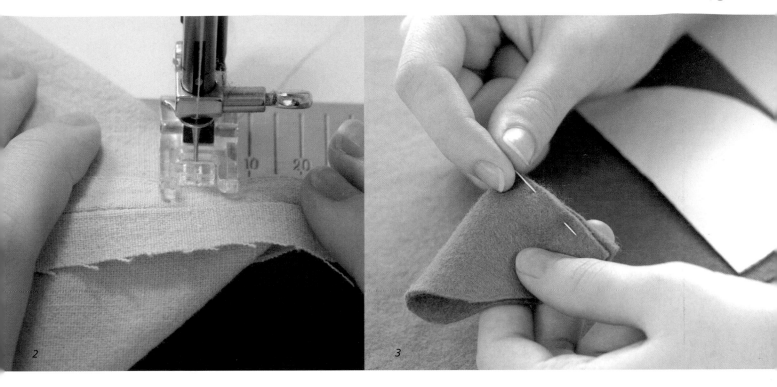

2

3

step two

With the bag still wrong-side out, fold the corners so
that the seam of the short side aligns with the seam or
fold on the long side. This will form a triangular point
at each corner as shown in the photograph above.
Stitch a straight line across the corner at a right angle
to the seams, 1in (2.5cm) from the point.

Trim off the pointed corners 5/8in (1.5cm) from the
stitching line. Turn the rectangle of fabric right-side
out through the opening in the long side seam. Hand
stitch the opening closed.

Fold the bag in half and press the fold. Open it out,
then fold the top part of the bag inside the lower part
so that the top half forms the lining and the lower half
the outside of the bag. Press carefully, taking particular
care around the top of the bag.

step three

Trace the half-circle template from page 142 onto
thin card or template plastic and cut it out. Lay the
template on the purple felt and trace around it with a
pencil, fabric marker or tailor's chalk. Trace and cut out
two semicircles of felt – one for each bunch of grapes.
Fold the semicircle in half as shown in the photograph
above. Pin and stitch along the straight edge to form
a cone shape. Turn the cone right-side out.

4

step four

Beginning at the tip of the cone, use beading thread and a long beading needle to attach purple beads to the felt. Work around the cone in a circular fashion, adding each bead beside the previous one.

After you have added a round of beads, check that there are no obvious gaps that need to be filled with an extra bead before you move on to the next round. Adding a few extra beads in the gaps between rounds will keep the bunch looking natural. There is no need to keep the rounds perfectly straight.

Continue adding beads until there is just ¼in (6mm) of felt visible at the round edge of the cone.

step five

Place a small amount of polyester fiber fill inside the felt cone. Use beading thread to make a row of running stitches around the top edge of the cone, without knotting either end of the thread. Gather the top edge of the cone slightly by drawing up the running stitches. Take the green cord and tie a knot in each end of the cord to prevent fraying. Slip the knot inside the top of the cone and draw up the running stitches tightly around the cord, hiding the knot and the edges of the felt inside the cone. Tie off the beading thread and thread both ends into the beading needle. Use the ends of the thread to stitch four or five leaf-shaped beads to the top of the bunch of grapes. Secure the ends of the thread with two small back stitches through the felt, then pass the thread through the bunch of grapes to hide the loose ends.

step six

Cut a 12in (30cm) length of green craft wire for each bunch of grapes. Wind the wire loosely around a pencil as shown in the photograph above. Slip the coiled wire off the pencil and stretch out the coils a little to make realistic vine tendrils.

Wrap the middle coil around the green cord near the top of the bunch of grapes. Bend the coiled ends of the wire into a pleasing curve. The wire should stay in place, but a couple of tiny stitches will help secure it.

snowdrop table linen

The texture on this elegant napkin and placemat comes from pulled-thread embroidery.

Snowdrops are a welcome harbinger of warm weather. These spring bulbs emerge soon after winter is over and their fresh, white flowers are examples of simple beauty. Snowdrops make appropriate subjects for embroidery: the simple structure of the blooms and the leaves give clean lines in a design.

materials and techniques

Pulled-thread embroidery is an excellent way of adding texture to a design. The stitches are worked by counting the threads of the evenweave fabric, then pulling the thread tight to create lace-like holes. If you have not done pulled-thread embroidery before, practice on scraps of fabric to get your tension correct.

Set a stylish table with hand embroidered linen.

snowdrop placemat
& napkin

materials

(Quantities are for one placemat and one
or two napkins)
17¾in x 55in (45cm x 140cm) of 28-count linen
in olive green
1 ball DMC pearl cotton no. 5, very light fern
green (524)
1 ball DMC pearl cotton no. 8, very light fern
green (524)
1 ball DMC pearl cotton no. 8, ecru
Machine sewing thread
2B lead pencil
Tapestry needle, no. 26
Basic sewing equipment (see page 122)

step one

From the linen, cut a piece of fabric measuring 16in x 20in (40cm x 50cm) for the placemat and a 17¾in (45cm) square for the napkin. Using machine sewing thread and running stitch, baste the outline of a rectangle measuring 13¼in x 18¾in (34cm x 47.5cm), in the center of the linen for the placemat. Baste the outline of a 16in (39.5cm) square in the center of the linen for the napkin.

Using pearl cotton no. 8 in very light fern green, work buttonhole stitch (see page 129) four threads long and one thread wide within the basted outline to create the hem of the placemat. At the corners, fan the stitches around by stitching into the same hole for several stitches. You may find it easiest to remove the basting as you go, to avoid stitching it into the finished embroidery. Leave the excess fabric outside the hem until all the stitching for the napkin is complete.

2

Measure in 1in (2.5cm) from the inside edge of the buttonhole hem, and baste a line for the border. Enlarge as indicated and trace the patterns from pages 142–3 onto the lower right-hand corners of the placemat and napkin with the pencil, either using a light box or by taping the pattern and fabric to a sunlit window. Baste over the pencil lines with machine sewing thread, to make the design easier to see on the fabric.

Stitch the border using ecru pearl cotton no. 8. Work two lines of satin stitch (see page 135), with each stitch over four threads. Leave gaps in the satin stitch where the leaf design crosses the border. Make sure the stitches are pulled tight. In the corners, step the stitch length down to mitre the corner: stitch over four threads, then three, then two, then one thread. Turn the corner and stitch over one thread, then two, then three, then four threads. Continue stitching over four threads along the next side of the border.

step two : napkin

Using pearl cotton no. 8 in very light fern green, fill leaf N1 with cable stitch, over three threads. See page 57 for a diagram of this pulled-thread stitch. Any small gaps in the stitching at the edges of the leaf where you can't fit another full stitch will mostly be covered with the chain-stitch edging. Once the leaf is filled, stitch the outline in chain stitch, using the same thread.

Using pearl cotton no. 8 in very light fern green, outline leaf N2 with stem stitch. Using pearl cotton no. 5 in very light fern green, stitch the leaf in padded satin stitch over the stem-stitch outline. Keep the tension firm but not tight.

Using pearl cotton no. 8 in ecru, fill the snowdrop stem and flower with honeycomb stitch, over two threads. See page 57 for a diagram of this pulled-thread stitch. Outline the flower and stem shape with chain stitch, using the same thread.

3

step three: placemat

Using pearl cotton no. 8 in very light fern green, fill the area of leaf P2 with wave stitch, over four threads. See opposite for a diagram of this pulled-thread stitch. Once the leaf is filled, stitch the outline in chain stitch, using the same thread.

Using pearl cotton no. 8 in very light fern green, fill leaf P4 with cable stitch, over three threads. Outline the leaf in chain stitch, using the same thread.

Using pearl cotton no. 8 in very light fern green, fill leaf P7 with single faggot stitch, over three threads. See opposite for a diagram of this pulled-thread stitch. Outline the leaf in chain stitch, using the same thread.

Using pearl cotton no. 8 in very light fern green, outline leaves P1, P3, P5 and P6 in stem stitch. Using pearl cotton no. 5 in very light fern green, stitch the leaves in padded satin stitch, as you did for leaf N2 on the napkin.

Using pearl cotton no. 8 in ecru, fill the snowdrop flower and stem with honeycomb stitch, over two threads. Outline the flower and stem shape in chain stitch, using the same thread.

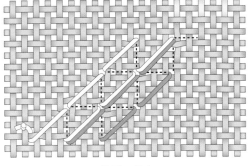

Cable stitch

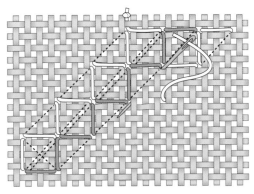

Faggot stitch

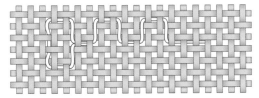

Honeycomb stitch

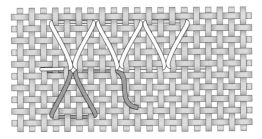

Wave stitch

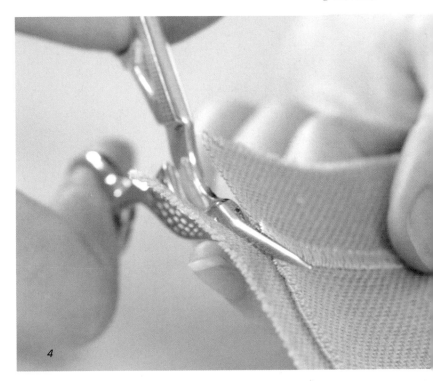

4

step four

If you have not yet removed your tacking threads, do so now. Once all stitching is complete, cut the excess fabric away from the outside of the buttonhole hem, taking care not to cut any of your stitches.

Press the napkin and placemat from the back of the work, using a hot steam iron and a pressing cloth. After hand-laundering, you may find it helps to press the linen while it is still slightly damp. Place the almost-dry linen in the freezer for 15 minutes before pressing for a crisp, crease-free finish.

spider orchid tea-cosy

Felt is a great insulator that will keep your favorite beverage hot in the pot.

Hot tea is enjoying a resurgence in popularity as a beverage, with many flavored blends adding to the enjoyment of this refreshing brew. To make a proper pot, add one teaspoon of leaves for each drinker and one for the pot. Add boiling water and allow the tea to draw for five minutes. Don't forget to turn the pot three times clockwise and once anticlockwise to stir the brew before you pour it out.

materials and techniques

Making your own felt is a simple process. The main special need for the task is a flat worktop that will cope with the small amount of mess involved. Merino fleece is available from selected craft shops, or you could try a search of the internet to find your nearest supplier.

Keep tea hot with this beautiful felted cosy.

spider orchid tea-cosy

materials

7oz (200g) fine white merino fleece

1oz (20g) coloured merino fleece in pink, green
and brown

1oz (20g) coloured silk tops in pink, green, brown

Bubble wrap for pattern piece

4–5 cups lukewarm water

¼ cup of laundry soap flakes or 1 tablespoon
of mild dishwashing detergent

Spray bottle

Two sheets of plastic, such as disposable painter's
dropsheets

Length of dowel or plastic pipe

Towel and string

Basic sewing equipment (see page 122)

step one

Enlarge the pattern from page 144 and cut it out of
bubble wrap. Divide the merino fleece into two equal
piles for the front and back of the cosy. Lay a plastic
sheet on your work table and place the pattern on top.
Place some pink fibres in the top triangular part of the
pattern. These will be covered with white fleece.
Take the white merino fleece in one hand. With the
other hand, pull out a small wisp of fiber and place it
on the bubble wrap. Build up a layer of fibers over the
whole pattern. Repeat, laying the fibers at a 90 degree
angle to the first layer.
Create the orchid design, using small wisps of coloured
fleece carefully placed on top of the white fleece. Add
silk tops to the coloured fleece to enhance the design.
Make up a solution of lukewarm water and laundry
soap or mild detergent.

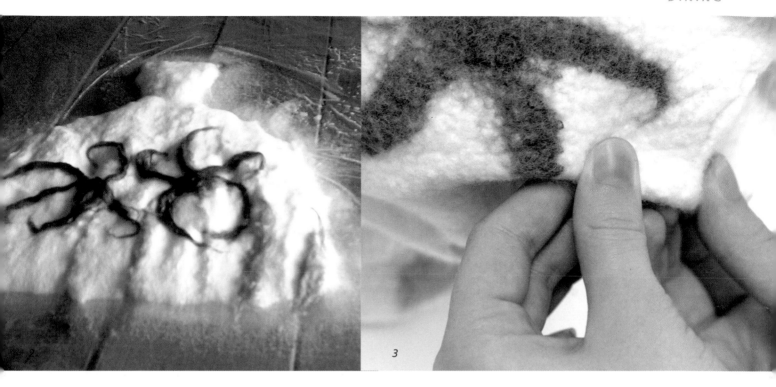

step two

With the soapy water in the spray bottle, spray the fleece
with a gentle mist until the wool fibers are thoroughly wet.
Place the second plastic sheet over the wool. Gently rub over
the plastic to ensure that the fleece is wet through.

Turn the piece over and remove the first layer of plastic. Fold
the ends of the fleece fibers over the sides of the bubble-
wrap pattern. Layer the white merino fleece on this side of
the pattern as in step one, then add the coloured fibres to
repeat the spider orchid design. Wet thoroughly with soapy
water as before and replace the plastic sheet.

Place the dowel or pipe on the near edge of the fleece
shape and roll the plastic and tea-cosy around the pipe. Roll
it up in towel and tie the roll firmly. Roll the tea-cosy firmly
backwards and forwards 200 times. Unroll the cosy turn the
pipe 90 degrees and roll it all up again. Continue rolling and
turning until the wool fibers are firmly felted together.

step three

Remove the plastic and gently throw the tea-cosy onto a
table. Turn it over and throw it again: it will start to shrink.
Continue until the cosy fits the pot it is intended for.
Rinse the tea-cosy thoroughly to remove any soap
solution. Cut along the lower edge of the tea-cosy and
remove the bubble wrap from inside. Cut slits in the
sides for the teapot handle and spout.

To create the flower on top of the cosy, tie a thread
around the narrowest part of the triangle. Cut the top
of the triangle and cut down to the tied thread to create
petal shapes. Pull the petals out and down.

Repeat the throwing process to enable the cut edges
to felt. Use your fingers to shape the tea-cosy and
top flower into the final shape. Leave the cosy to dry
completely. Lastly, remove the thread from the base
of the flower.

two for tea

Use your quilting and appliqué skills to make this simple tea-cosy.

"Tea, though ridiculed by those who are naturally coarse in their nervous sensibilities... will always be the favourite beverage of the intellectual," said Thomas De Quincey in his *Confessions of an English Opium-Eater.* A hot pot of this refreshing draught is the perfect accompaniment to morning or afternoon snacks, and a padded tea cosy allows you to extend the delightful experience by keeping the liquid hot for longer.

materials and techniques

Starting with a basic 10in (25cm) square shape, your imagination can go to town when you decorate the tea cosy. On the following pages you will find instructions for an appliqué teapot motif. You could also try using a traditional patchwork block, or making a crazy patchwork shape. A monogram like the one that has been used on the bedlinen on page 76 would make an elegant embroidery choice.

Once you have selected and decorated your tea-cosy fabric to your satisfaction, the assembly is quite basic: simply make a sandwich of fabric, batting and lining and stitch it together at strategic points to leave room for the handle and spout.

There is nothing like a tea-cosy for setting a tempting table.

two for tea

materials

10½in x 21in (26cm x 52cm) cream
jacquard-weave fabric
20in (50cm) green hand-printed fabric
10½in x 21in (26cm x 52cm) cotton fabric
such as calico for lining
10½in x 21in (26cm x 52cm) thin quilt batting
9in (23cm) square of pink fabric for appliqué
9in (23cm) square of double-sided fusible
interfacing (also known as appliqué paper)
Pencil
Stranded embroidery cotton in a color to match
or contrast with the appliqué fabric
Crewel needle, no. 9
80in (2m) double-sided satin ribbon,
1in (2.5cm) wide
Basic sewing equipment (see page 122)

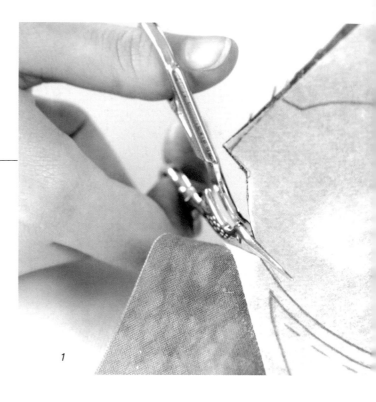

1

step one

Cut the jacquard fabric into two squares measuring 10½in (26cm). Trace the shapes for the teapot appliqué (see page 144) onto the paper side of the double-sided fusible interfacing, then follow the manufacturer's instructions to iron the interfacing onto the wrong side of the pink fabric. Carefully cut out the shapes on the traced line. The dashed lines on the template show where the pieces are to be overlapped.

Measure 3¼in (8cm) up from the lower edge of the jacquard fabric square and position the teapot body so that it sits on this line. Remove the backing paper and carefully position the spout and handle of the teapot so that the parts indicated by the dashed lines are tucked under the edge of the main teapot shape. Put the teapot lid piece in place and carefully fuse the shapes to the jacquard fabric following the manufacturer's instructions.

2

step three

Cut the lining fabric and quilt batting in half to give two 10½in (26cm) squares of each. Place the outer fabric and the lining fabric with right sides together and lay them on top of the quilt batting. Pin all the layers together and stitch a ⅜in (1cm) seam along the lower edge. Trim the batting close to the stitching and turn the fabrics to the right side with the quilt batting sandwiched between them. Pin and baste around the three remaining edges, ⅜in (1cm) from the edge.

To angle the corners, measure 2⅜in (6cm) from the corners along the top and side edges of the cosy. Use a pencil or tailor's chalk to draw a line across the corner between these points. Baste along this line. Cut off the corner ⅜in (1cm) from the marked line.

From the remaining print fabric, cut bias strips 1⅜in (3.5cm) wide. See page 128 for instructions. Join the strips until you have two lengths of at least 32in (80cm) each. Press one long edge of the bias strips under by ⅜in (1cm). Lay a strip right-side down on the front of the tea-cosy, aligning the raw edges. Beginning from the lower left edge, turn a small hem on the bias strip and stitch along the basted line through all layers. When you reach the lower right corner, trim off the excess bias strip and turn under a small hem before you finish stitching. Turn the pressed edge of the bias strip to the back of the tea-cosy piece and hand stitch the edge to the existing line of stitching. Repeat with the other bias strip for the back of the cosy.

Lay the back and front pieces of the cosy together with wrong sides facing. Pin and hand stitch them together on the binding line, starting 1in (2.5cm) below the corner. Stitch around the top of the cosy and down the other side, finishing level with your starting point.

Cut the ribbon into four equal lengths and use slip stitch to attach one length to each side edge of the front and back of the cosy, level with the printed fabric seam.

step two

Using two strands of embroidery cotton and a crewel needle, stitch around the raw edges of the appliqué shapes in buttonhole stitch (see page 129). First work around the outer edges of the spout and handle, then around the main body of the teapot. Finish by working blanket stitch right around the lid. Press the work from the back.

Cut two 4in x 10½in (10cm x 26cm) pieces of printed green fabric for the bottom strip. Set the remaining printed fabric aside for now. Press a ⅜in (1cm) seam allowance to the wrong side of the fabric, then open it out. Place the seam allowance of the printed fabric right-side down on the right side of the tea cosy front, aligning it so that the pressed seam allowance sits just below the appliqué teapot on the front, and in the same position on the back. Pin and stitch along the pressed line. Fold the strip of printed fabric down and press the seam flat.

hands & hearts

Add a modern twist to traditional chicken-scratch embroidery by working with the woven designs on ready-made tea towels.

Kitchen essentials for drying dishes and hands, cotton or linen tea towels are also a complement to your kitchen décor. Modern woven designs such as stripes, country-style checks and waffle weave can easily be decorated with stitching to add a unique style.

materials and techniques

Chicken-scratch embroidery is sometimes known as Amish embroidery or Depression lace. Traditionally worked on gingham and checkered fabrics, the basic stitches are snowflake stitch, which looks like an asterisk; running stitch or straight stitch; and lace stitch (four straight stitches with thread wrapped around the centre). The designs here use adapted stitches because they are larger than usual: the snowflake stitch is couched down in the center to anchor it, while the lace stitch is worked as separate straight stitches rather than with the thread wrapped around the centre. For instructions on working these stitches in the traditional way, see pages 130–1.

Bring warmth to a country kitchen with unique tea towel designs.

hands & hearts

materials

*Ready-made cotton or linen tea towels with
striped or checkered patterns*

*1 skein each of two contrasting colors of DMC
pearl cotton No. 5*

Crewel needle, no. 8

Masking tape or ruler

Tailor's chalk, pencil or fabric marker

Basic sewing equipment (see page 122)

step one

If the tea towel you have selected has a checkered
pattern, use the squares as the guide for your stitching.
Otherwise, you will need to make marks at regular
intervals across the stripes to keep your stitches even.
Using the width of the woven stripes as an indication
of the size of the stitches, cut a strip of masking tape
to the same width as two stitches (two stripes). Lay the
strip of masking tape across the stripes at the hem of
the tea towel and mark the position of the first stitches
on the opposite edge. Remove the masking tape and
replace it above the marks, then mark the position of
the second row of stitches above it. Repeat along the
length of the stripes.

step two

See page 145 for layout diagrams of the two designs featured on these pages.

Using one of the embroidery threads in a contrasting color, work snowflake stitch (see page 131) on the two outer stripes or, if using a checkered tea towel, in every other dark colored square as shown in the photograph on page 66. If the stitches will be quite large to cover the woven design on the tea towel, work a short couching stitch over the center of the snowflake to anchor the threads.

step three

Using the second contrasting embroidery thread color, work lace stitch (see page 130) between the snowflakes. The photograph shows a modified version of lace stitch because the stitches are larger than normal. The traditional stitch shown on page 130 comprises four straight stitches worked across the light squares, with the thread wrapped around the central ends of the straight stitches to form a diamond shape in the dark square. Larger stitches will sit flatter if they are worked as straight stitches between the points of the outer stitches, rather than wrapping the thread around them. Continue stitching until the design is complete. The tea towel may be laundered in a gentle wash and pressed from the back between uses.

tea time treat

Good coffee is like friendship: rich and warm and strong.

Many have written of the warm feeling that comes from sharing a cup of tea or coffee with a friend. The words embroidered around this cloth have come to us from generations past: Chinese and Russian proverbs, witticisms from humorists, lines of poetry and even advertising slogans based on a subject that warms the cockles of your heart.

materials and techniques

The lettering is stitched in simple back stitch in a chocolate thread to contrast with the coffee-colored evenweave cloth. The tablecloth can be a ready-made one, or you can make your own by simply hemming a square of evenweave fabric to the dimensions of your tea table.

If your table is not square, simply extend the square to an oblong to fit and add a few of your own favourite quotations about food and drink.

Set the table for afternoon tea and set the mood for friendship and delight with these homely quotations.

tea time treat

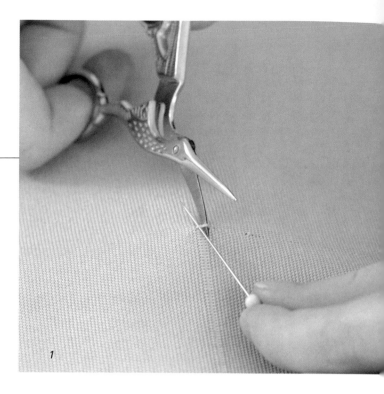

materials

*6ft (180cm) square 22-count evenweave
    tablecloth (for 3ft or 90cm square table)*
*3 skeins DMC stranded cotton in dark beige
    brown (839)*
*1 skein DMC stranded cotton in medium beige
    brown (840)*
Crewel needle, no. 9
Sharp-pointed embroidery scissors
Basic sewing equipment (see page 122)

step one

Fold the tablecloth into quarters and measure 17in
(42.5cm) from the center point along the two sides. Mark
this point on each side with a pencil or tailor's chalk, then
open and refold the cloth to mark the remaining side.
Spread out the cloth on a flat surface. Measuring along
the straight grain of the fabric through the marked
points, mark the corners of a 34in (85cm) square in the
centre of the cloth. Carefully snip a single thread in each
direction at one corner of the square, then use a pin to
tease the end of the thread out of the fabric until you
have enough thread to grip and pull. Draw the thread up
gently until you can see where it meets the next corner
mark, and snip the thread at that point so that you can
remove it completely from the cloth. Repeat on the three
remaining corners.

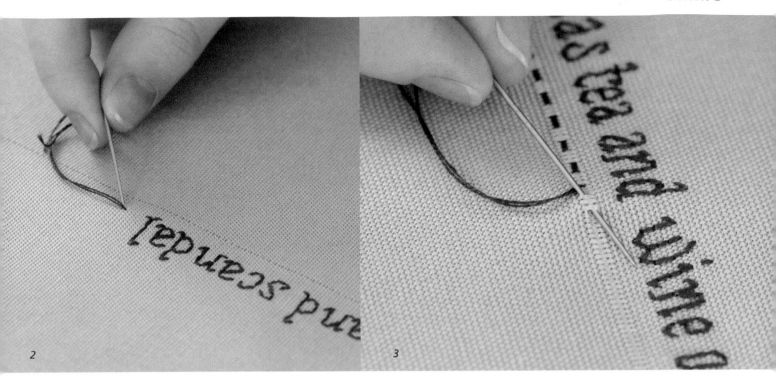

2

3

step two

Begin stitching at one corner, four threads inside the drawn thread line. The first quotation begins: "Good coffee is like friendship". A selection of appropriate quotations to fit this sized cloth is featured on page 145. Using two strands of stranded cotton in dark beige brown (839), work the capital letter G according to the chart on page 146. Stitch the outlines of the capital letter in back stitch over two threads of the tablecloth fabric. Fill in the upright lines of the capital letters with cross stitches. Leave two threads of the fabric between letters and four to six threads between words. Continue stitching the letters of the quotation in back stitch over two threads according to the chart. Use a cross stitch as a full stop and a cross stitch with a straight stitch tail as a comma. Instructions for working cross stitch and back stitch can be found on pages 129–37.

step three

Change to two strands of stranded cotton in medium beige brown (840) and use the smaller capital letters in the chart to stitch the source of the quotation. Continue stitching the quotations along the sides of the center square. When you approach a corner, you may need to add an extra thread space between letters or a couple of extra thread spaces between words to ensure that there is not too large a gap at the corner, or a word that bends in the middle! When you get to the last quotation, count the remaining threads to make sure you have enough space to finish it and reduce or increase the number of threads between letters accordingly. Finish the design by working a row of running stitch around the square in two strands of dark beige brown threadxe, filling in the gap left by the drawn threads. Stitch over and under three fabric threads for each stitch.

bed & bath

Celtic knots

Crisp white cotton pillowcases are complemented by a neatly embroidered monogram.

A monogram consists of a person's initials and, traditionally, it was the initial of the surname or family name that took prominence. The status of having a family pedigree, a name with a reputation in the community, took precedence over the individual's given name. These days, it's more likely that a monogram will focus on the initial of a person's first name, as monograms are seen as a way of personalising something, or labelling it as the property of an individual.

materials and techniques

You can embroider a monogram onto ready-made sheets and pillowcases or make your own bed linen from cotton sheeting, which is readily available in fabric stores. White embroidery on white sheeting is traditional, but self-colored embroidery on colored sheeting can also look elegant. White embroidery on colored sheeting is another option, or, for a real visual statement, try a dark, colorfast thread such as red or black embroidery on white sheeting. The only no-no is any kind of patterned or striped fabric: the embroidery will just be visual clutter.

Turn your bed into a rich resort by adding simple monograms to the pillowcases.

Celtic knots

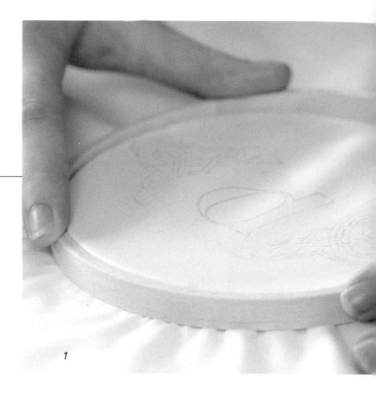

1

materials

*20in x 65in (50cm x 165cm) white cotton
    sheeting (for each pillowcase)*
DMC pearl cotton no. 12, white (Blanc)
Crewel needle, no. 9
6in (15cm) embroidery hoop
Water-soluble fabric marker
Basic sewing equipment (see page 122)

step one

Fold over 29³⁄₈in (74.5cm) of fabric, then a further
28¾in (73cm). There should be 6⅞in (17.5cm) left over
in the last section. Press the folds and stitch a line of
basting along the creases. In the top left corner of the
centre panel, which will be the front of the pillowcase,
measure 4¾in (12cm) down from the top edge and
3¼in (8cm) in from the fold line. Center the letter
of the monogram at this point.

Enlarge the letter for your monogram and the Celtic
knot design from page 147 and use a water-soluble
fabric marker to trace it onto the fabric: trace the letter
first, marking the dotted line as well, then line this up
with the dotted line on the Celtic knot design and trace
the knots on both sides of the letter. Always follow the
manufacturer's instructions when using a water-soluble
marker. Place the fabric in an embroidery hoop.

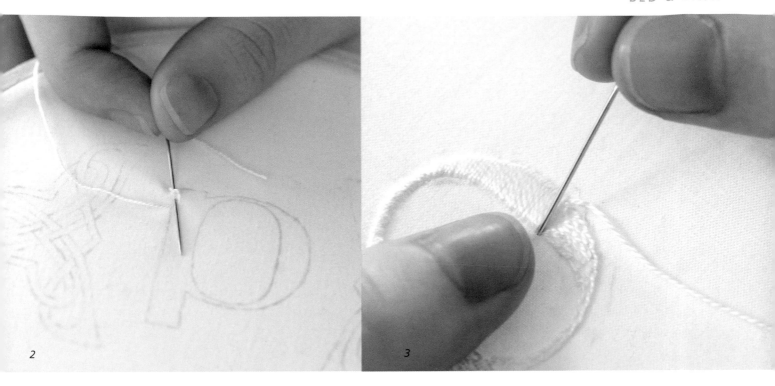

2

3

step two

The embroidery for the monogram is worked with white pearl cotton no. 12 thread and a no. 9 crewel needle. Work the monogram letter in padded satin stitch. See page 135 for instructions on working padded satin stitch. Stitch a line of chain stitch just inside the traced outlines of the letter. Work one line of chain stitch in the narrow hoizontal parts of the letter. In the wider vertical parts, several rows of chain stitch are required to fill the area completely. Continue working lines of chain stitch until the letter shape is completely filled.

step three

Work the satin stitch over the rows of chain stitch. The Celtic knot work is stitched in shadow stitch, using very small stitches. Shadow stitch looks like back stitch on the front and herringbone stitch on the back. See page 135 for instructions on working shadow stitch. When you have finished the embroidery, wash out the water-soluble marks following the manufacturer's instructions. To make up the pillowcase, hem each end of the material by folding in a ¼in (6mm) double hem and stitching it down. Fold the fabric along the basted lines, with right sides together for the main body of the pillowcase. Fold the short flap under the centre panel with wrong sides facing, so the fabric forms a zigzag. Stitch through all layers down both long sides, then turn the pillowcase right side out and press carefully. Use a pressing cloth to cover the embroidery.

sheer delights

A pretty fleur-de-lys design in shadow stitch decorates an organza curtain.

Sheer curtains soften harsh daylight and add a romantic touch to your bedroom décor. Sheer curtains, unlike heavy drapes and upholstery, are inexpensive and easy to update to change the mood in your interior decorating scheme. To add a personal touch, some pretty embroidery is just the ticket.

materials and techniques

Shadow work is ideal for sheer fabrics, as the stitching on the back of the fabric shows through to the front. Traditionally worked in white on white, the shadow work stitch is also known as double back stitch. See page 135 for details on how to work the stitch.

Fluttering in the breeze, these light and pretty curtains set a fresh mood for your interior décor.

sheer delights

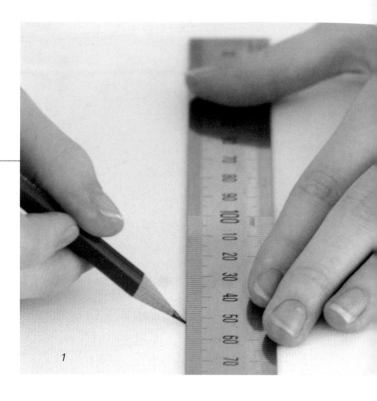

1

materials

Cream organza ready-made curtain

*1 skein each of DMC stranded cotton, very dark
    raspberry (777) and dark forest green (987)*

Crewel needle, no. 9

Beading needle, no. 15, or fine sharps needle

Monofilament thread, clear

25 clear glass, silver-lined seed beads

Embroidery hoop

Bias tape (optional)

*Sharp HB pencil, tailor's chalk or other temporary
    fabric marker*

Basic sewing equipment (see page 122)

step one

Using a sharp pencil or the temporary fabric marker
of your choice, trace the pattern from page 148 onto
the curtain. Each motif should sit 6in (15cm) above the
hemmed edge of the curtain. Space five motifs evenly
across the width of the curtain.

Mount the first motif in the embroidery hoop. The
organza slips through the hoop very easily and can be
readily pulled out of shape. If this happens, tightly wrap
the inner hoop with strips of bias tape. Finish off the
end of the tape with a few stitches to hold it in place
and mount the embroidery.

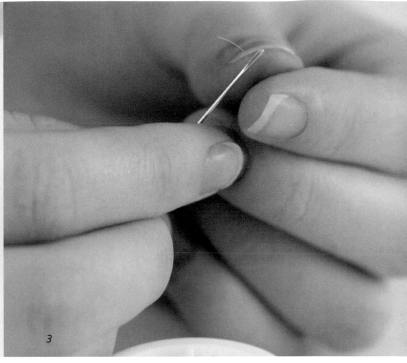

step two

Work the embroidery in shadow stitch, using a very short back stitch. Try to keep stitches to a maximum of ⅟₁₆in (1.5mm) in length. Using one strand of embroidery thread, work the top lozenge of the motif in very dark raspberry (777), and the two lower curlicues in dark forest green (987).

Instructions for working shadow stitch can be found on page 135. To start stitching, use a waste knot: knot the thread and stitch it into the right side of the fabric a couple of inches from the motif. When the stitiching is finished, weave the thread through the back of the stitching, along one side of the shape. If you weave the thread tails under the center of the stitching, they will be visible from the front. Cut off the waste knot, thread the tail of thread into the needle and hide the beginning of the thread in the same way.

step three

Using the beading needle or a fine sharps needle and the clear monofilament thread, sew five seed beads down the center of each pink lozenge shape. Make sure the monofilament thread is well anchored in the back of the nearby stitching.

Carefully press the curtain using the appropriate settings on the iron. Organza may be woven from silk, rayon or synthetic fibres so check the curtain's label for proper care instructions. Avoid the beads and monofilament thread when ironing.

art nouveau rose

Guests will be delighted to dry their hands with this pretty embroidered linen towel.

The art nouveau movement used stylised natural forms with elongated lines, asymmetric ornamentation and exotic imagery. Well-known art nouveau designers include Charles Rennie Mackintosh, René Lalique and Louis Tiffany. Mackintosh's roses were the inspiration for the design on this simple linen handtowel, which evokes the style and manners of yesteryear.

materials and techniques
Linen is an excellent fabric to use for a hand towel as its absorbent properties are about 50 per cent greater than cotton. Linen can be laundered in the same way as cotton, although handwashing of this towel is recommended to ensure the embroidery isn't damaged.

An embroidered linen handtowel looks too pretty to be used.

art nouveau rose

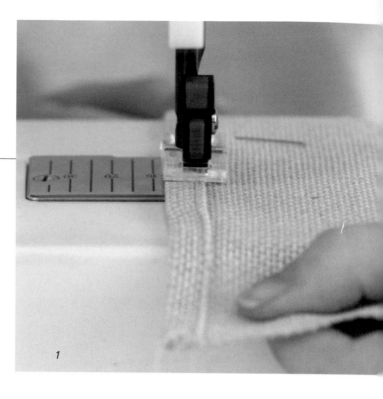

1

materials

*16in x 23½ in (40cm x 60cm) natural linen,
      25 count*

*1 skein each of Anchor stranded embroidery
      cotton in very light blue–green (213),
      light pistachio green (214), medium pistachio
      green (215), very light shell pink (968),
      light shell pink (969) and very dark shell
      pink (970)*

Crewel needle, no. 7

Water-soluble fabric marker

Embroidery hoop

Machine sewing thread to match linen

Basic sewing equipment (see page 122)

step one

Prewash the linen so that the fabric will not shrink after
the embroidery is complete. Along the long sides, fold
in a ⅜in (1cm) double hem. Baste in place. Along the
short sides, fold in a ¾in (2cm) double hem. Baste in
place. Machine stitch the hems, ¹/₁₆in (2mm) from their
inside edge, using matching sewing thread.

Enlarge the pattern on page 148. Place the fabric
over the pattern, and match the lower hemmed
edges of the towel with the dotted guidelines. Use a
water-soluble fabric marker to trace the embroidery
design onto one end of the handtowel (use a light box
or tape both the pattern and towel to a sunlit window).
Use the water-soluble fabric marker in accordance with
the manufacturer's instructions.

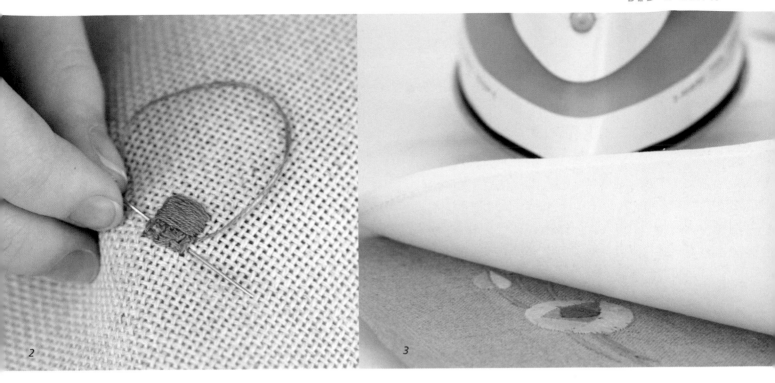

2

3

step two

Stitch the entire design in padded satin stitch. See page 135 for instructions on working this stitch. Work all stitches using three strands of embroidery cotton and the no. 7 crewel needle.

Outline all the shapes in chain stitch and fill in the shapes. For the stems, work a single line of chain stitch down the center. Work satin stitch over the top of the chain stitch stitching into the outlines of each shape. Work the stems in medium pistachio green (215), the upper half of each leaf in very light blue–green (213) and the lower half in light pistachio green (214). Work the outer petals in very light shell pink (968), the center in very dark shell pink (970), and the areas in between in light shell pink (969). The squares on each side of the design have the darkest pink shade innermost, then the medium shade and the lightest shade on the outer squares.

step three

Remove the basting. Rinse the fabric well in cold water to remove the water-soluble fabric marker (always follow the manufacturer's instructions). Allow the towel to dry until it is only slightly damp and place it in the freezer for 10–15 minutes before ironing. Lay the towel face down on thick towels and press the back with a steam iron, using a pressing cloth as shown in the photograph.

lavender's blue

A sprig of embroidered lavender on cotton reveals the contents of these scented sachets.

Perfect to give as a small gift on many occasions, a lavender bag can be added to a drawer to softly perfume socks and smalls. You can leave one under your pillow to help induce sleep. The strong smell of lavender makes it a favourite with many; however, dried rose petals, geranium leaves and other herbs also make lovely scented gifts.

materials and techniques

Fine cotton poplin or lawn is the best fabric for a lavender sachet, as the light fabric allows the aroma to escape while keeping the tiny dried flowers inside. These little bags can be made in many shapes and sizes and filled as much as you like. They can also be used as a presentation bag for scented soaps and other small gifts. The whimsical heart design is an alternative you can use if the contents of the bag will not be lavender-scented.

Keep a collection of scented sachets on hand to give as thank-you gifts and for other occasions.

lavender's blue

materials

7in x 10in (18cm x 25cm) cream poplin fabric for
each sachet

1 skein each of DMC stranded cotton, variegated
lavender (52), light khaki green (3013)

Two small buttons (for the heart motif)

16in (40cm) cream satin ribbon, 1/8in (3mm) wide
for each sachet

Crewel needle, no. 9

Small embroidery hoop

Pencil or water-soluble fabric marker

Cream machine sewing thread

Basic sewing equipment (see page 122)

1

step one

Fold the fabric in half across the shortest dimension,
giving a rectangle 5in x 7in (12.5cm x 18cm), with a
fold down one side. Press the fold, then open the fabric
out. Work the embroidery in the center of one half of
the fabric, 1½–2in (4–5cm) from the lower edge.
Place the fabric upside down in an embroidery hoop,
so that it sits flat on your work surface with the right
side up, as shown in the photograph above. Trace the
pattern from page 148, using a pencil or water-soluble
fabric marker. There are two patterns to choose from:
a sprig of lavender or a vine heart.

To make a bunch of lavender like the one shown on
page 74–5, trace the sprig three times with the stems
crossing over. Trace only two leaves on the outside
stems and add a wavy line at the crossover point to
represent string tying them together.

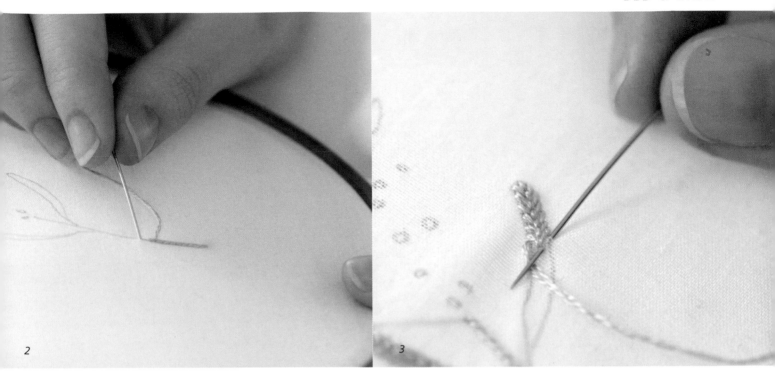

2

3

step two

It is not necessary to trace every tiny circle for the lavender flowers. Trace just a few of the outer ones to suggest the shape, or simply draw the outline of the flower head.

Remove the fabric from the embroidery hoop and re-stretch it over the inner hoop, right-side up. Work the embroidery with the fabric the right way up in the hoop, as shown in the photograph above. Embroider the stem of the lavender on the traced line, using two strands of light khaki green thread and outline stitch. For stitch instructions, see page 134.

step three

Work the leaves of the lavender in fly stitch. See page 132 for instructions on working this stitch. Begin at the tip of the leaf with a short, straight stitch, then work fly stitches very close together in a row. Make the legs of each stitch touch the previous stitch. The anchoring straight stitches will run down the center of the leaf like a vein.

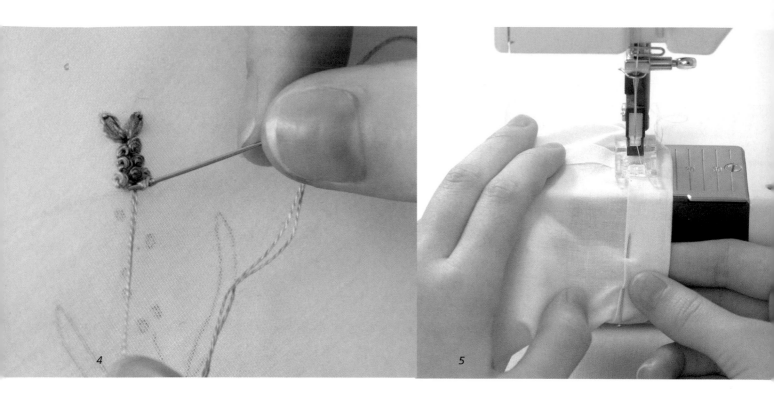

4

5

step four

Make two lazy daisy stitches at the top of the lavender
flower, using two strands of variegated lavender thread.
See page 133 for instructions on working lazy daisy
(detached chain) stitch.

Make French knots with three wraps of thread,
beginning at the top of the flower and placing the
knots close together. See page 132 for instructions
on working French knots. If you need to begin a new
length of variegated embroidery thread, turn the new
pair of strands around when you thread the needle,
so that the shade at the beginning of the stitching
is similar to the shade you have just finished with.
This will ensure that there is no sudden change in the
variegated color.

step five

When the embroidery is complete, remove the fabric
from the hoop and press gently from the back. Place a
towel under the embroidery so that you don't flatten
the French knots.

Fold the fabric in half with the right sides together. Pin
and stitch a seam across the base of the sachet and up
the raw side edges to create a bag. Use a 3/8in (1cm)
seam allowance. Clip the corners diagonally at the base
of the bag.

Turn a double hem at the top of the bag, 3/8in (1cm)
wide. Pin and machine stitch along the edge of the
hem. Turn the sachet right-side out and press from the
back. Fill the little bag with dried lavender, soap or the
aromatic material of your choice and tie it closed with
a length of satin ribbon.

6

step six

For the heart motif variation, you can stitch the motif
entirely in light khaki green or variegated lavender.
The colour scheme shown in the photograph has
the outline in light khaki green and the flowers in
variegated lavender.

The heart shape itself is worked in outline stitch. The
stems of the leaves and flowers and the curls of the
vine are worked in back stitch (see page 130). The
flowers are made up of three lazy daisy stitches. The
leaves are also lazy daisy stitches, worked in reverse;
that is, beginning the stitch at the tip of the leaf and
making the anchoring stitch one of the back stitches
on the stem. Use two strands of embroidery cotton
throughout this design.

Add two small buttons as indicated in the pattern
on page 148.

just for you

made with love

Make a gift more personal with a handmade card.

Your family and friends will love the card as much as they love the gift it accompanies. These simple designs don't take long to stitch, so you can make anyone's special day more perfect.

materials and techniques

The tiny cross-stitch designs on these cards were inspired by quilt blocks. They are worked on 18-count evenweave fabric to fit neatly into the 2in (5cm) square window in the card. If you use fabric with a different thread count, the designs will be larger or smaller, so the cards and windows will need to be cut to different sizes. Note that the higher the thread count, the smaller the design will be.

Say thank you, happy birthday or congratulations in stitches with these mini cards.

made with love

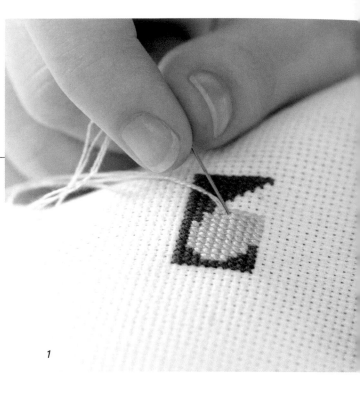

1

materials

3in x 9in (7.5cm x 22.5cm) colored cardboard, for
*   each card*

5in (13cm) square of white or cream 18-count
*   Aida fabric, for each card*

DMC stranded cotton in colors indicated on the
*   charts on pages 148–9*

Tapestry needle, no. 24 or 26

½in (12mm) wide double-sided adhesive tape

Cutting blade

Ruler and pencil

Cutting mat

Basic sewing equipment (see page 122)

step one

Starting in the center of the square of Aida fabric,
stitch the cross-stitch pattern by following the chart
on page 148 or 149. For instructions on working cross
stitch, see page 131.

Work all of the embroidery in the colors indicated in
the chart, using two strands of cotton and a tapestry
needle. Start and finish threads by running them under
the back of the stitches, rather than using a knot.
Once the embroidery is complete, press the piece
carefully from the back.

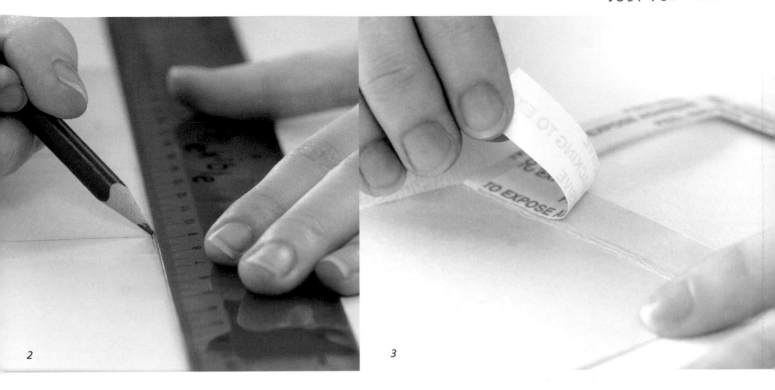

2

3

step two

Use a cutting blade to lightly score the card 3in
(7.5cm) from each end. Fold the card on the scored
lines, then open it out again.

Use a pencil to mark a 2in (5cm) square window in the
middle of the center panel. Use the cutting blade to
cut it out carefully, working on a cutting mat.

step three

Lay double-sided adhesive tape along each edge of the
window, inside the card.

Trim the Aida fabric so that there is a ½in (12mm)
border around the edge of the cross-stitch design.
Place a tiny piece of double-sided adhesive tape on the
wrong side of the fabric in the center of the design,
to hold it still while you complete the next step in
assembling the card.

4

North Star: nice for Christmas

step four

Place the design right-side up on the inside of the left-hand section of the card. Make sure the edges of the design are parallel with the edges of the card, then bring the window lightly over the top to check the alignment. Adjust the position of the stitched design if necessary, then press the window down over the cross-stitch design.

Open out the left-hand panel and detach the tiny piece of adhesive. Place more double-sided adhesive tape on the back of the fabric, around the edges. Replace the tiny piece in the center with a longer strip. Fold the left-hand panel of the card back over the fabric and press it down firmly. Write your message on the inside of the right-hand panel.

Medallion: Congratulations

Tulip: to express your thanks or wishes

Hearts: for Valentine's day

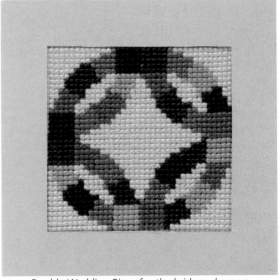

Double Wedding Ring: for the bride and groom

amethysts to cherish

For a special occasion, this elegant beaded necklace will set off your evening gown perfectly.

Making your own jewellery is not difficult. This beaded collar is strung together using a beading needle and thread, with no other special equipment or skills required to create a masterpiece.

materials and techniques

The glass beads used in this jewellery are not real gemstones, of course. However, carefully selected cut crystals can make mere glass look like much more. Seek out your local bead supplier for both beads and fixings. If you purchase the quantities given overleaf, you should have enough materials left over to make a bracelet and earrings or a brooch as well.

Light dances on the facets of Czech cut glass beads.

amethysts to cherish

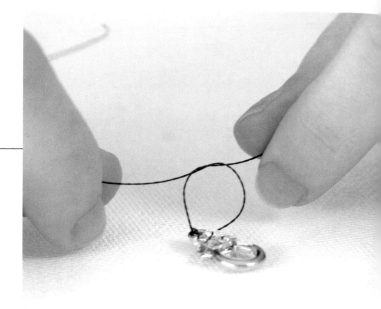

1

materials

Beading thread, white

Beading needle

Gold lobster clasp and jump ring

Clear nail varnish

3oz (60g) of 3mm Indian round glass beads, amethyst

2oz (40g) of 5mm Czech cut crystal faceted beads, clear AB

2oz (40g) of 6mm Czech round crystal beads, clear with gold swirls

20 Czech crystal leaf beads with holes at the top end, 3/8in (10mm) long, mauve

Forty 4mm brass bicone beads

Twenty 3mm brass cylinder beads

Extra gold lobster clasp and jump ring (bracelet)

Two gold earring hooks

1 dozen amethyst seed beads (bracelet and earrings only)

Scissors

step one

Cut a length of beading thread 3yd 10in (3m) long. Be careful to avoid tangles in the thread as you work. It is important to have the thread long enough so that you can complete the entire necklace with one strand. Tie the thread through the ring at the base of the lobster clasp with a firm knot. Leave a 4in (10cm) tail at the start of the thread. Place a tiny dab of clear nail varnish on the knot to ensure that it does not loosen. Note that we have used black beading thread in the photographs for clarity. The actual necklace was created with white thread.

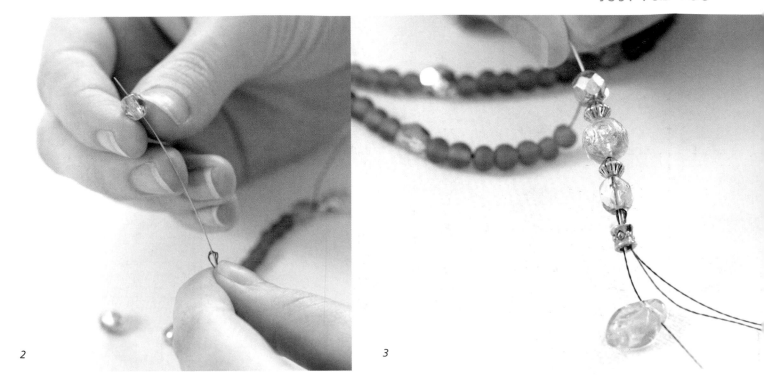

2

3

step two

Thread the beading needle with the long end of the
beading thread. Create the inner circle by placing one
Czech cut crystal faceted bead on the needle, followed by
seven amethyst Indian glass beads. Slide the beads along
to the end of the thread near the lobster clasp. Repeat
the bead pattern (faceted bead, seven amethyst glass
beads) 11 more times and finish with a faceted bead.
Pass the beading needle and thread twice through an
8mm jump ring and make a secure knot. Place a tiny dab
of clear nail varnish on the knot to ensure that it does
not loosen. Pass the needle and thread back through the
last faceted bead.

Place seven amethyst glass beads on the beading needle
and slide them along the thread. Add a faceted bead and
seven more amethyst glass beads.

step three

Make the drops at the edge of the collar by adding beads
in the following order: faceted bead, brass bicone bead,
round crystal swirl bead, brass bicone bead, faceted bead,
brass cylinder bead, mauve crystal leaf bead.

When the beading needle and thread have passed
through the leaf bead, push all the beads along the thread
so they sit close to the previous strand of beads. Return
the beading needle and thread through the beads for the
drop in reverse order, as shown in the photograph. The
leaf bead anchors the drop. Work back up to the inner
circle of the necklace by adding seven amethyst glass
beads, a faceted bead, then seven amethyst glass beads.
Pass the needle and thread through the faceted bead in
the centre of the first row, then add seven amethyst glass
beads. See the diagram on page 106 for details.

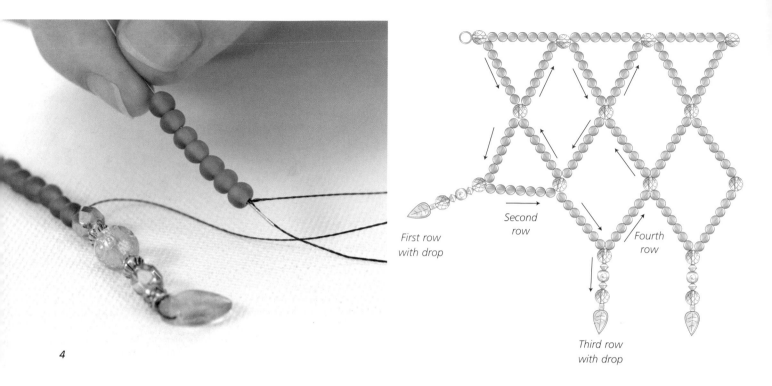

4

First row
with drop

*Second
row*

*Third row
with drop*

*Fourth
row*

step four

Pass the beading needle and thread through the next
faceted bead in the inner circle of the necklace. Add seven
amethyst glass beads, a faceted bead, seven amethyst glass
beads, pass the needle and thread through the second
faceted bead in the previous row, add seven amethyst glass
beads, then make another drop as in step three.

Continue in this manner until you reach the last row. Bead
the last row to match the first row. Finish off the beading
thread by knotting it securely through the lobster clasp ring.
Cut the end of the thread to 4in (10cm). Thread both tails,
from the beginning and end of the work, into the beading
needle and pass the beading needle through the first two
sections of the inner circle of beads. Cut off the thread
close to the beads.

Place a drop of clear nail varnish on the new knot in the
lobster clasp ring.

bracelet and earrings

You should have enough beads left over to make a matching
bracelet and earrings, as shown in the photograph. The
beading pattern for the bracelet is a seed bead, five amethyst
glass beads, faceted bead, brass bicone bead, round crystal
swirl bead, brass bicone bead, faceted bead, seed bead, leaf
bead, seed beed, faceted bead, brass bicone bead, round
crystal swirl bead, brass bicone bead, faceted bead, five
amethyst glass beads, faceted bead, brass bicone bead, round
crystal swirl bead, brass bicone bead, faceted bead, seed
bead, leaf bead, seed bead, faceted bead, brass bicone bead,
round crystal swirl bead, brass bicone bead, faceted bead, five
amethyst glass beads, seed bead.

The beading pattern for the earrings is a seed bead, three
amethyst glass beads, and then the same drop design as for
the necklace. Take the beading thread all the way back to the
top and tie a secure knot through the loop of the earring hook.

evening glamor

A swish of silky crepe with a touch of glittering gold is the perfect accessory for a night at the opera.

The elegant outfits suitable for special occasions call for accessories that complement their style. It's no use throwing any old cardigan over a designer-label dress if the night air is a little chilly. This shawl and matching silk purse are so quick and easy to make, you could make several in different colours to match all your outfits.

materials and techniques
The embroidery design is a simple version of a curvaceous paisley swirl, giving a slightly retro feel to the shawl. It's meant to be worked freehand on a sewing machine, so there's no elaborate tracing or embroidery stitches.

Dress up an evening outfit with this gorgeous shawl and purse.

evening glamor

materials

25in x 58in (63.5cm x 147.5cm) cream crepe
  fabric

9in x 40in (23cm x 102cm) cream silk dupion
  fabric

9in x 20in (23cm x 51cm) lightweight polyester
  batting

Madeira Metallic thread, no. 20, gold (2024) and
  no. 40, gold (gold-6)

Cream sewing thread

1 dozen Maria George gold flower sequins, 5/8in
  (1.5cm) diameter

Large press stud or flat skirt hook and eye

Pencil, tailor's chalk or water-soluble fabric marker

Basic sewing equipment (see page 122)

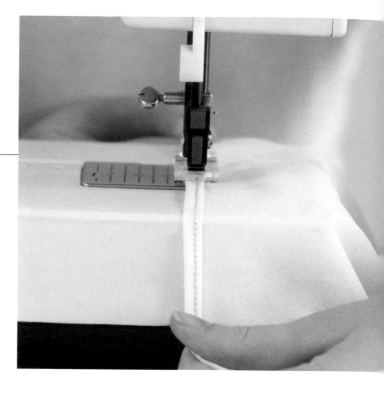

step one

Cut any selvedges off the piece of cream crepe fabric. If your sewing machine has a hemming attachment, make use of it. A hemming attachment is a special sewing machine foot with a curl of metal that rolls the fabric as it is fed under the needle. It makes an even, narrow, double hem.

If you don't have a hemming attachment, pin a narrow double hem (⅛in or 3mm) and stitch it by hand or machine using cream sewing thread.

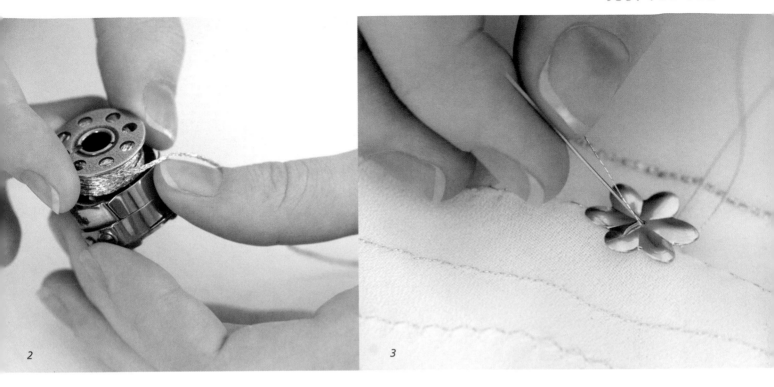

2

3

step two

When working with metallic threads in your sewing machine, stitch from the wrong side of the fabric with the metallic thread in the bobbin and normal sewing thread in the top of the machine. Wind the Madeira Metallic no. 20 gold thread onto the bobbin of your sewing machine and thread the machine with cream sewing thread.

Look at the design on page 148. Draw a freehand outline of the paisley shape on the wrong side of the fabric with a pencil, tailor's chalk or a water-soluble fabric marker. You can draw some of the internal lines or simply stitch them freehand once you have the outline in place.

Place the shawl right-side down in the sewing machine. Using a straight stitch, stitch around the outline of the paisley shape. Stitch three more echoes of the outline inside the shape, about 2in (5cm) apart.

step three

Change to Madeira Metallic no. 40 gold thread in the bobbin. Use straight stitch, zigzag and any other fancy stitches that your sewing machine offers. Stitch echoes of the paisley shape between the previous stitching lines until you are happy with the design. Lay the shawl out on a flat surface and scatter the flower sequins over the design. Stitch the sequins to the design using no. 40 gold thread. Stitch them on the machine stitching lines and weave the ends of the thread into the back of the stitching so there are no loose ends of thread.

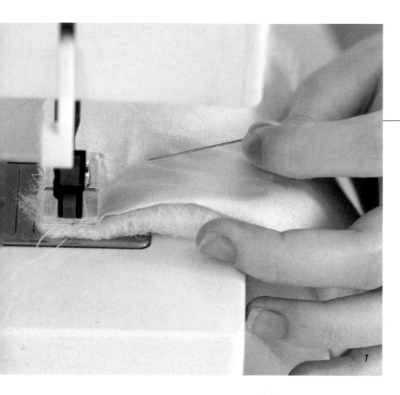

clutch purse

step one

Draw or trace the paisley design at one end of the silk dupion, on the wrong side of the fabric. The design should be placed 1in (2.5cm) from the end and the sides and should be no wider than 5in (12.5cm). Stitching from the wrong side of the fabric, machine embroider the paisley shape as for the shawl.

Fold the piece of silk dupion in half with wrong sides together, sandwiching the batting in between. Lay the sandwich so that the embroidered end is face down. Measure 6in (15cm) from the folded edge and fold this section over onto the top of the sandwich. Carefully bring the embroidered section of the fabric out from underneath and fold it back over the top so that the raw edges meet. You should now have a layer of batting and two layers of fabric with right sides together at the top end. At the other end, there should be a layer of batting, two layers of fabric with right sides together, another layer of batting and another two layers of fabric with right sides together.

Pin all the layers together. With the sewing machine threaded with ordinary sewing thread in the bobbin and on top, stitch all of the layers together down one long side of the purse. Use a ³⁄₈in (1cm) seam allowance. Stitch the other side and part of the way across the end of the purse, leaving an opening for turning.

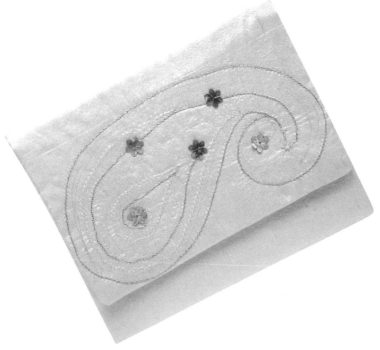

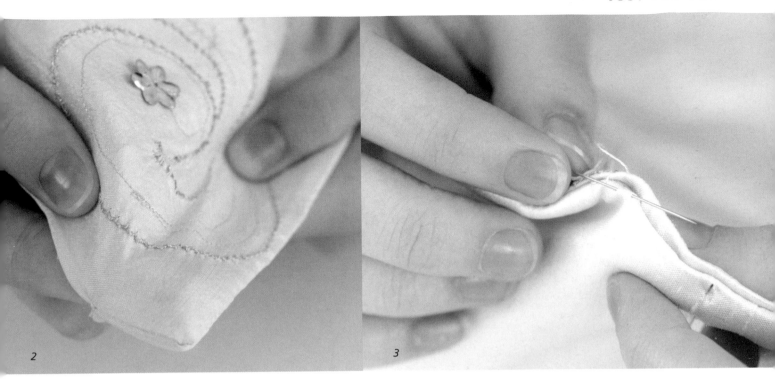

2

3

step two

Clip the corners diagonally. Trim the batting close to the stitching line. Turn the purse right side out through the opening. When you do this, you will find that the folded part of the purse forms the pocket of the purse and the embroidered end forms the flap.

Before you sew up the opening, place flower sequins on the embroidered design and stitch them down using Madeira Metallic no. 40 thread. Hide the ends of the thread inside the purse.

step three

Attach the male side of a large press stud or the hook part of the skirt hook and eye to the underside of the embroidered flap, using cream sewing thread. Close the flap to work out the position for the female side of the press stud or the eye of the skirt hook and eye on the front of the purse pocket and stitch it in place. Stitch the opening closed using ladder stitch. See page 133 for instructions on working ladder stitch.

beautiful buttons

Buy a button kit at your craft store and create unique embellishments for clothing, soft furnishings and other items.

Embroidered buttons like these could be used in many decorative situations. In the photograph at left, they are used for the closure on a felt journal cover. You could also use them as embellishments on cushions and quilts. You could even use them to turn a cardigan or blouse into an original fashion statement.

materials and techniques

Button-making kits are available at haberdashery stores. The kits usually contain the requirements for six buttons. There will be six caps and six shanks, plus a rubber holder and a plastic pusher. Instructions are included, but the photographs over the page will help you as well.

Tiny embroidery stitches cover buttons with leaves and flowers.

beautiful buttons

materials

6in x 9in (15cm x 22.5cm) cream homespun
    fabric

DMC stranded cotton, variegated green (94)

Crewel needle, no. 9

2B pencil

$^5/_8$in (1.5cm) button kit, six buttons

Basic sewing equipment (see page 122)

1

step one

Using a button cap from the kit as a template, draw
around the circumference onto the fabric, angling the
pencil slightly out from the button cap as shown in the
photograph. This will ensure there is enough fabric to
cover the sides of the button cap.

Button 1

Button 2

Button 3

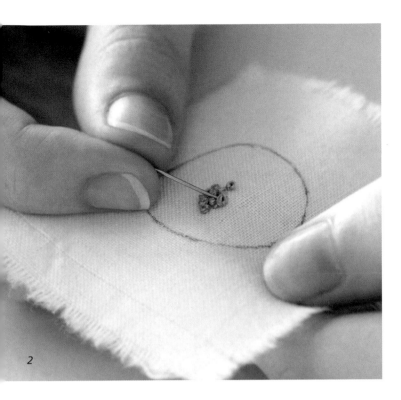

2

step two

Work the embroidery inside the circle, using two strands of thread and a no. 9 crewel needle. Use any combination of your favorite embroidery stitches to achieve good coverage right to the edges of the circle. See pages 129–37 for instructions on working embroidery stitches. The stitches used on the buttons are as follows:

Button 1: French knots, three wraps. Begin in the center and work a loose spiral of knots to the outer edge. Work back along the spiral, placing knots in the corners between the previous ones. Continue until the entire circle is covered.

Button 2: Lazy daisy flowers with French knot centers. Start with a five-petalled flower in the center, then work flowers around it in the gaps between the petals. Work another row of flowers around this to cover the entire circle.

Button 3: Feather stitch. Work from one edge of the circle to the other, filling in with more branches on each side until the entire circle is covered.

Button 4 (overleaf): Lazy daisy stitch. Starting with a French knot in the center, work lazy daisy stitches radiating out from the knot. Work rows of radiating lazy daisy stitches until the entire circle is covered.

Button 5 (overleaf): Outline stitch. Starting with a French knot in the centre, work a spiral of outline stitch out to the edge of the circle. Work another spiral alongside the first, then another spiral until the entire circle is covered.

Button 6 (overleaf): Running stitch. Starting with the outside edge of the circle, work tiny running stitches around the perimeter. Work rings of running stitch towards the center of the button, keeping the stitches and gaps between them even. If the stitches start to line up with each other, work a few stitches with longer gaps between them.

Button 4

3

Button 5

step three

Place the embroidery face down in the button holder cup that came in the kit. Align the edges of the circle with the edges of the holder. Press the metal button cap into the holder with your finger, keeping the embroidery as even as possible.

The kit should also include a pusher like the yellow one shown in the photograph. Place this evenly over the button cap and push down firmly.

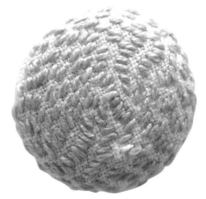

Button 6

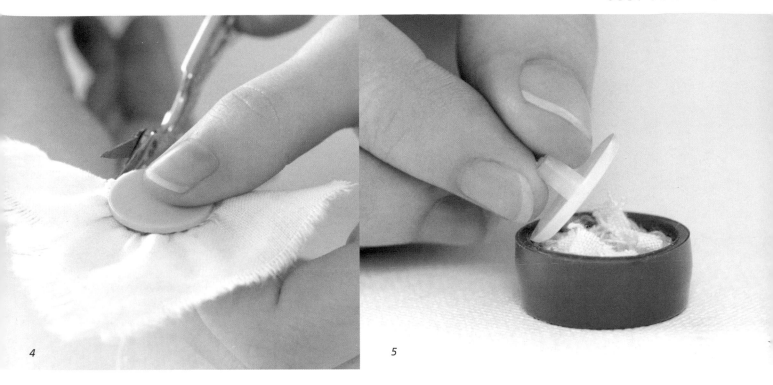

4

5

step four

Hold the pusher and holder in one hand and use small scissors, such as embroidery scissors, to trim away excess fabric. Use the outside of the holder as a cutting guide. Trim away all but 1/8in (3mm) around the outside of the pusher.

step five

Take the pusher out. Use your fingers to fold the edges of the fabric over the edges of the metal button cap. Place the plastic button shank into the holder and push it down firmly with the pusher.

To remove the button from the holder, push it out from underneath while bending the walls of the holder slightly.

Sew the button in place on the journal cover, cushion or item of clothing you want to decorate.

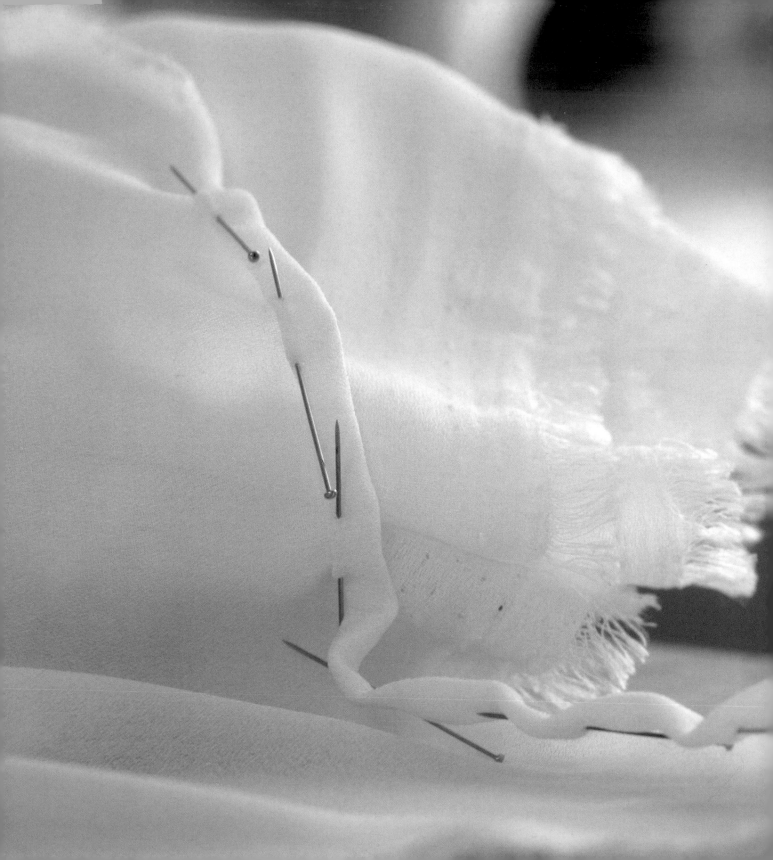

tools & techniques

basic sewing equipment

This list of essential accessories will ensure you've got the right tools at hand for the projects in this book and many other stitching tasks.

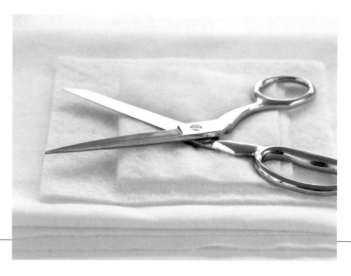

Fabric scissors.
Do not use fabric scissors to cut paper or other materials, as this will blunt the blades more quickly.

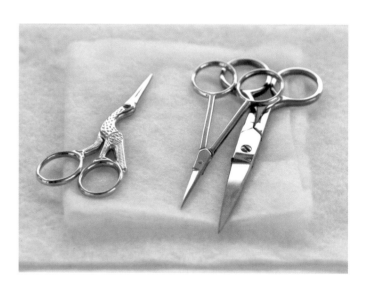

Scissors.
A pair of embroidery scissors with sharp points for snipping fine threads and small stitches is essential: stork scissors are a popular and decorative choice, but plain scissors do the job just as well. A pair of medium-sized, multipurpose scissors are handy for cutting paper patterns and other jobs.

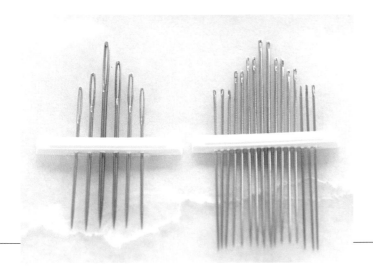

Sewing needles.

A selection of different sizes is a good start. Most of the projects in this book will specify a size and style of needle, so you will soon add to your basic collection. There are several types of needle:

• Crewel needles are sharp pointed needles with small eyes, suitable for embroidery and other hand sewing.

• Tapestry needles have a large eye and a rounded point, for working on evenweave fabric.

• Chenille needles have a large eye and a sharp point, and are suitable for silk ribbon embroidery and working with textured threads.

• Straw needles have a small, round eye and the eye end is the same diameter as the shaft.

• Betweens needles are short, fine needles suitable for hand quilting.

• Beading needles are extra fine needles that will easily pass through the center of beads.

Sewing thread.

Start your collection with cotton and polyester thread in black, white and ecru. Other colours can be purchased to match fabrics for your projects.

Pins.

Choose good quality, steel-plated pins with fine shafts. Start with basic fine steel pins and add quilting pins, silk pins and any others you require for your projects as necessary.

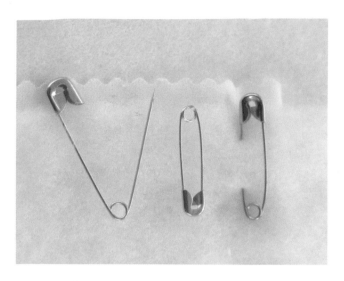

Safety pins.

A selection of sizes will come in handy for many tasks, including fastening project pieces together so they don't get separated from each other and lost.

Water-soluble fabric marker or tailor's chalk.

Both of these are easily removed from fabric. A sharp HB or 2B pencil can be used instead.

Thimble.

This may seem somewhat old-fashioned but after you've pricked your finger a few times you'll wish you had one!

Sewing machine.

A basic machine that is capable of straight stitching as well as zigzag and buttonhole stitching is all you will need for the projects in this book. If you've never used a sewing machine before, read the manufacturer's instructions carefully.

Iron and ironing board.

Most households are equipped with this essential. A steam iron with settings for the various fabrics you will be using is a good investment. A pressing cloth is another good investment: you can find these at your local craft supply store.

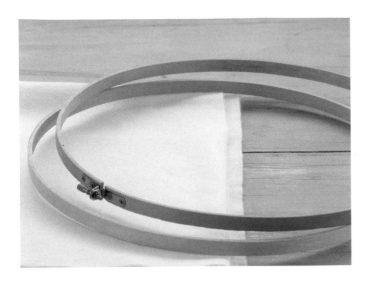

Embroidery hoop.

A hoop is useful for keeping the fabric taut while you work embroidery stitches. Hoops are available in many sizes: a 6in (15cm) diameter is a good first hoop as it is easy to hold.

Rotary cutter and mat.

The very sharp circular blades on this useful tool allow accurate cutting of fabric in straight lines when combined with a quilter's ruler (below left). A self-healing cutting mat is its essential partner to protect your work surface and the blade. Used mainly by quilters, you may find them useful for other sewing projects.

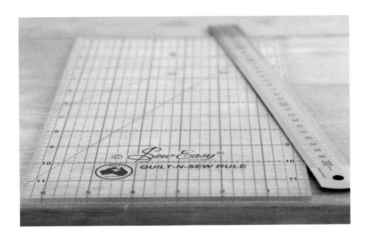

Rulers.

A clear Perspex quilter's ruler with markings in inches as well as angled cutting lines can be very useful. A metal ruler is an alternative you can use with a rotary cutter. A tape measure is also useful in your tool kit.

basic techniques

The techniques demonstrated on these pages are used in some of the projects in this book.

fusible appliqué

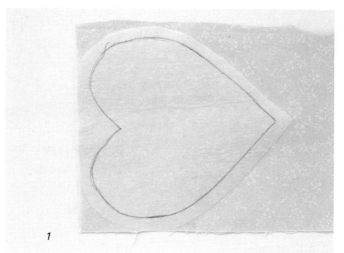

1

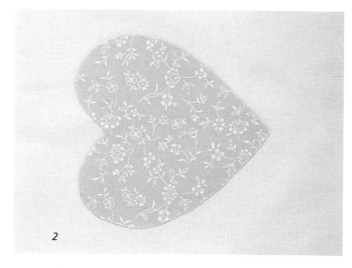

2

step one

Draw or trace the shape onto the paper side of
the double-sided fusible interfacing (also known as
appliqué paper). Note that a non-symmetrical shape
must be reversed when traced, so that it will be the
right way around when the appliqué is fused.

Cut the shape out roughly, about ¼in (6mm) from
the traced line. There is no hem allowance on fusible
appliqué, as the fusing process prevents fraying.

Lay the fusible interfacing shape, paper side up, on
the wrong side of the appliqué fabric. Following the
manufacturer's instructions, press with an iron to fuse
the interfacing to the fabric. Cut out the appliqué
shape on the traced line.

step two

Remove the paper backing, exposing the fusible
interfacing on the wrong side of the appliqué shape.
Lay the shape right-side up, in position on the
background fabric. Carefully press with an iron to
fuse the two fabric layers together.

Complete the appliqué by stitching around the outer
edge of the appliqué shape using buttonhole stitch.
See page 129 for instructions on working this stitch.

cutting on the bias

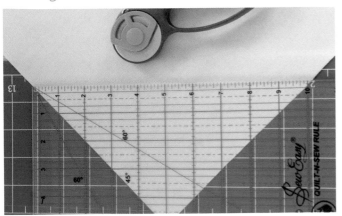

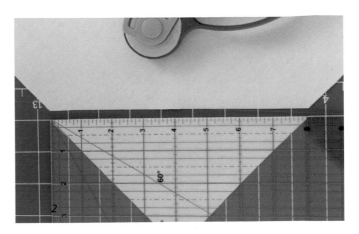

step one

Remove the selvedges of a piece of fabric and ensure that the edges are cut straight along the warp and weft of the fabric. Place the fabric on the cutting mat. Align the 45 degree line on the quilting ruler with one edge of the fabric.

step two

Slide the rotary cutter along the edge of the quilting ruler to cut through the fabric.

(If you do not have a 45 degree line on your ruler, fold the fabric so that the top edge aligns with the side edge and press the diagonal fold. Make your first cut along this fold.)

step three

Cut strips of the desired width parallel to the first cut. The strips in the photograph are 2½in (6.5cm) wide. Note that you can fold the fabric at right angles to the bias cut to allow you to cut longer bias strips. See page 128 for instructions on joining bias strips.

joining bias strips

step one

Binding can be cut on the bias or on the straight grain of the fabric. Even if you cut the strips on the straight grain, use a 45-degree bias seam to join them, as it reduces the bulk. Lay the strips at a 90 degree angle to each other. Pin and stitch a seam across the corner as shown in the photograph. Trim the seam allowance to no more than ¼in (6mm).

step two

Open out the binding strip and press the seam open. Trim off excess seam allowance fabric to make a straight edge along the strip. Continue joining strips until you have a single strip of sufficient length to go all the way around the quilt.

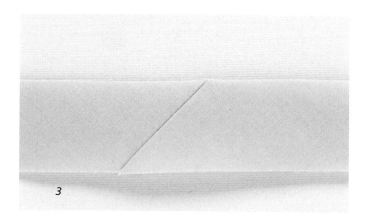

step three

Fold the binding strip in half lengthways, with wrong sides together. Press the fold to a sharp crease. Notice that the bias seam sits flatter than a straight seam, as the extra fabric in the seam allowance is spread over a larger area.

basic stitches

The projects in this book use the stitches illustrated on these pages. Refer to the project instructions for details such as the length of the stitch, the size and type of needle and the type of thread to use.

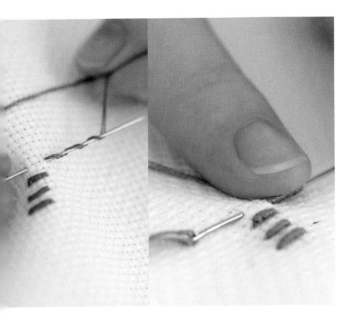

bullion stitch

Bullion stitch (sometimes called grub stitch) makes small, thick bars of embroidery thread on the surface of the fabric. The thickness of the stitch is created by wrapping the embroidery yarn around itself. Starting with a knot on the wrong side of the fabric, bring a straw needle out at one end of the position for the bullion stitch. Insert the needle at the other end of the bullion stitch position and bring out the point of the needle next to the tail of the embroidery thread. Wrap the tail of the thread around the needle several times. Five to eight wraps is usual, although it depends on the length of the stitch and the thickness of the thread. Push the wraps down the needle to the base and place your finger on top of them to hold them in place while you pull the needle through. Finish the stitch by returning the needle and thread to the back of the fabric through the same point that you originally stitched down through.

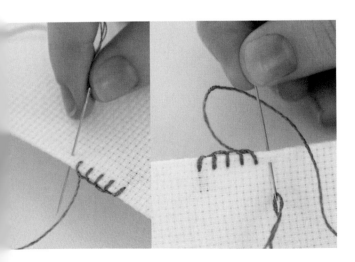

buttonhole (blanket) stitch

Buttonhole or blanket stitch is often used on the raw edges of fabric. In quilting, it is used for fusible appliqué. Starting with a knot on the wrong side of the fabric, bring the needle out at the edge of the fabric. Holding the loop of thread out of the way, place the needle back through the fabric at a point a little way across and down from the starting point. The actual distance will depend on the desired size of your stitches, which can be as large as you like.

Bring the needle to the front of the fabric at the raw edge. Ensure that it has passed through the loop of thread. Continue along the raw edges of the fabric in this manner until they are completely covered by stitching.

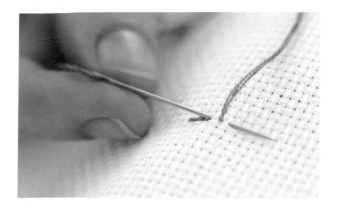

back stitch

Back stitch makes a solid line of stitching. It is often used to outline shapes, or to create lines. Starting with a knot on the wrong side of the fabric, bring the needle and thread to the front. Make a short stitch on top of the fabric, then another stitch the same length as the first underneath. Put the needle back into the fabric at the end of the first stitch and bring it out again another stitch length beyond the tail of the embroidery thread. Repeat.

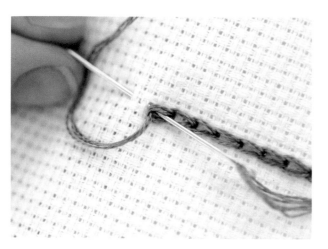

chain stitch

Starting with a knot on the wrong side of the fabric, bring the needle and thread to the surface of the fabric at the start of the line to be embroidered. Carry the thread around in front of the needle in a large loop. Insert the needle into the same place as the thread comes up, and bring the needle back to the surface one stitch length away. Make sure that it is inside the loop of thread. Pull the needle through the fabric. The loop should retain a rounded shape, but not be too loose. Work the next stitch in the same manner, making sure that the needle goes into the front of the previous loop.

chicken scratch: lace stitch

The legs and loops of this retro-style stitch give a lacy appearance to the gingham fabric on which they are worked. Begin with a knot on the back of the fabric and bring the needle and thread to the front of the work halfway along one side of a gingham square. Work four straight stitches, radiating out from the sides of a central square. Bring the needle and thread back to the surface beside the inside end of one of the legs of the cross. Carry the thread around in a circle, sliding the needle under the other straight stitches. Pull the thread to the inside ends of the legs; however, do not pull it so tight that it puckers the fabric. Take the needle and thread to the wrong side of the fabric through the same hole as it came up.

chicken scratch: snowflake stitch

This retro-style stitch is designed to be worked on gingham fabric. It is simply a double cross stitch. Begin with a knot on the back of the fabric and bring the needle to the front of the work at one corner of a gingham square.

Work straight stitches diagonally to form a cross. Now work straight stitches vertically and horizontally to form a star.

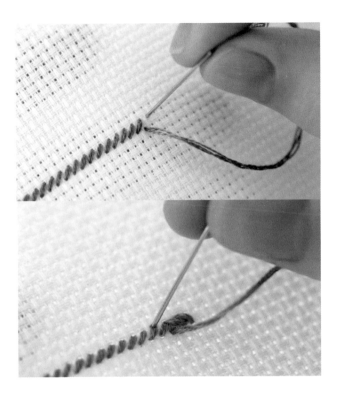

cross stitch

Cross stitch is a counted-thread stitch that is usually worked on evenweave fabric. The important thing to remember when working cross stitch is that the crosses should all go the same way. To do this, begin the first thread with a waste knot; that is, a knot on the front of the work some distance from the starting point. Once you have finished the first length of thread, cut off the waste knot and thread the tail under six or seven stitches on the back to secure it. Subsequent lengths of thread can be started by sliding the needle and thread through the back of six or seven of the previous stitches.

Stitch in rows and blocks of colour. Using a tapestry needle, begin by working the first diagonals of all the stitches in a row. On the back of the work, the stitches should all be vertical.

Return along the row, stitching the opposite diagonals over all the half-stitches you have made. The stitching instructions will indicate how many strands of embroidery thread you need to use as well as how many threads of the fabric you need to stitch over for each stitch.

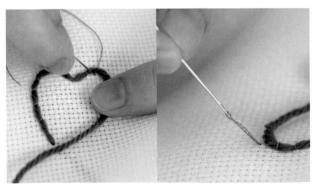

couching

Couching is stitching with a fine thread to hold a thicker yarn or decorative fiber to the surface of the fabric. To begin, lay the thick yarn on the fabric in the desired shape. Pin it in place if you wish. Thread a needle with a single strand of embroidery or sewing thread in a matching color.

Take short stitches across the yarn or fibre, holding it to the fabric in the desired shape. Start and finish the embroidery thread on the wrong side of the fabric.

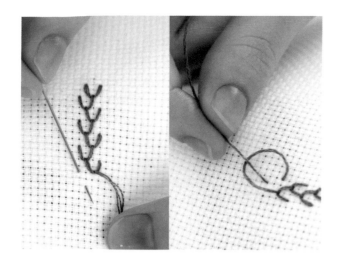

feather stitch

Knot the end of the embroidery thread and bring the needle and thread up from the wrong side of the fabric. Holding the loop of thread below the stitch with your thumb, put the needle back into the fabric 1/8–1/4in (3–6mm) to one side of the point where the thread emerges. Bring the needle to the front of the fabric at a point making an equilateral triangle with the previous two points, inside the loop of thread.

Pull the thread through to create a "U" shaped stitch. Holding the loop of thread below the stitch with your thumb, insert the needle 1/8–1/4in (3–6mm) from where the thread emerges, to the other side of the line of stitches. Bring the needle up to make a triangle as before, inside the loop of thread. Continue alternating from left to right sides of the center line.

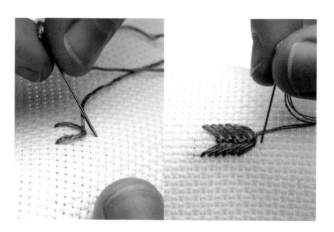

fly stitch

Starting with a knot on the wrong side of the fabric, bring the needle and thread to the front of the fabric. Holding the tail of the thread in a loose loop below the stitch, insert the needle into the fabric one stitch width from the starting point. Bring the point of the needle to the front of the fabric, at a point making an equilateral triangle with the previous two points. Ensure that the needle comes up inside the loop of thread.

Pull the needle through the fabric so that the tail of the thread holds the stitch in a "V" shape. The "leg" of the fly stitch can be as long or as short as you like. Many fly stitches worked in a row create a fern-like leaf.

french knot

French knots are small, round stitches that can be used to highlight designs, add details or fill a space with texture. Beginning with a knot on the wrong side of the fabric, bring the needle and thread to the front of the fabric. Choose a slightly larger needle than you would normally use for the thickness of the thread.

Wrap the thread around the needle (French knots commonly have two or three wraps). Holding the thread around the needle, insert the point of the needle next to the tail of the thread. Hold the wraps of thread with your thumb or finger as you pull the needle and thread through to the back of the fabric. Pull the knot gently to get a neat, firm finish.

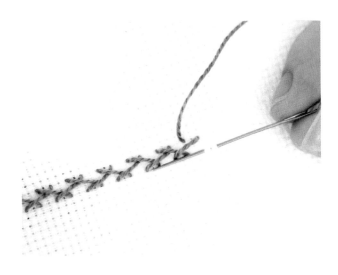

herringbone stitch

Herringbone stitch is a variation of cross stitch, with long legs that cross over each other. Begin with a knot on the wrong side of the fabric. Bring the needle to the front of the fabric. Stitch diagonally across the area to be embroidered, making the stitch twice as long as the width. Take the needle back on the wrong side of the fabric half the distance to the original starting point, on the opposite side of the stitching. Make a second diagonal stitch back to the original side of the stitching. Take the needle back on the wrong side of the fabric and bring it to the front level with the opposite leg of the previous stitch. Continue stitching in the same manner.

ladder stitch

Ladder stitch is used to invisibly join two pieces of fabric, particularly to close openings left after turning items right-side out. It gets its name because the stitches look like the rungs of a ladder. Beginning with a knot between the two pieces of fabric, bring a needle threaded with sewing thread to the edge of the fold on one piece of fabric. Stitch across to the other piece of fabric, taking the needle for a short distance through the fold. Stitch back across to the first piece of fabric. Continue stitching in this manner until the opening is closed.

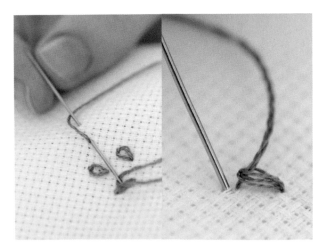

lazy daisy stitch (detached chain stitch)

This stitch is basically a single chain stitch. Starting with a knot on the wrong side of the fabric, bring the needle and thread to the surface of the fabric. Carry the thread around in front of the needle in a large loop. Insert the needle into the same place as the thread comes up, and bring the needle tip to the surface one stitch length away. Make sure that it is inside the loop of thread. Pull the needle through the fabric. The loop should retain a rounded shape, but not be too loose. Return the needle and thread to the wrong side of the fabric on the outside of the loop, making a small anchoring stitch.

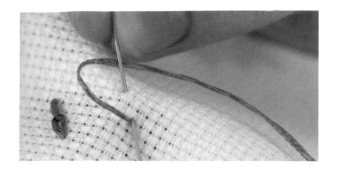

lazy daisy stitch (detached chain stitch) plus bullion stitch

Longer anchoring stitches on a lazy daisy stitch give a different effect. This variation of lazy daisy stitch has a bullion stitch as the anchoring stitch. Begin the lazy daisy stitch as described on the previous page, then work a bullion stitch — as described on page 129 — as the anchoring stitch.

long-and-short stitch

This stitch is often used as a filling stitch for larger areas of embroidery. Starting with a knot on the wrong side of the fabric, bring the needle and thread to the front of the fabric at one edge of the area to be filled. Work long and short stitches alternately along the edge of the area.

When you reach the end of the area, work back along the row. Bring the needle up at the end of the stitches of the previous row. Make the stitches in the second and subsequent rows even in length, to keep the long-and-short edge for the next row of stitching. Complete the area with a row of alternating long and short stitches.

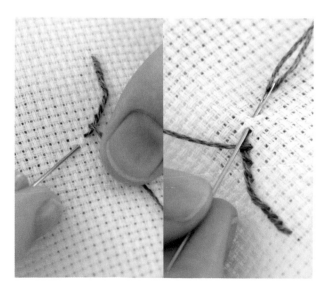

outline stitch

Begin with a knot on the wrong side of the fabric. Bring the needle to the front and work a short stitch (1/8in or 4mm long, for example). Bring the needle up halfway along the stitch. (Hold the loop of thread out of the way above the stitch as you stitch.) Pull the thread through, then work another stitch the same length as the first, this time bringing the needle up at the end of the first stitch. Continue in the same manner until the line of stitching is complete.

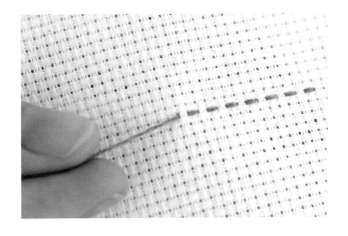

running stitch

The easiest stitch of all, running stitch is an embroidery stitch that can also be used to baste seams and quilts, and to gather fabric. Starting with a knot on the wrong side of the fabric, bring the needle and thread to the surface of the fabric. Take a stitch on the front, then a stitch on the back, then a stitch on the front.

With practice, you will find it easy to rock the needle in and out of the fabric for several stitches at a time. Stitches can be any length you like; you may also vary the length of the gaps between the stitches.

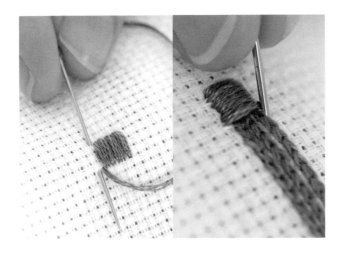

satin stitch

This decorative stitch is a simple way of filling areas with color. Bring the needle and thread to the front of the fabric. Stitch across the area to be filled, and bring the needle up again next to the starting point. Keep the stitches close together, so that they form a smooth, satiny surface. When you have finished filling the area with color, take the needle and thread to the wrong side of the fabric. Pass the tail of the thread underneath the stitching to finish it off.

For padded satin stitch, work a row of chain stitch (see page 130) around the outline of the area to be stitched. Fill in the space between the outlines with chain stitch. Work satin stitch over the chain-stitched outlines.

shadow stitch

Shadow stitch is sometimes called double back stitch, because on the front of the fabric it looks like two rows of back stitch. On the back of the fabric, the embroidery thread weaves back and forth between the two rows, filling in the middle with colored thread that shows on the surface of sheer fabric as a tint of color.

Begin with a waste knot and bring the needle and thread to the front of the fabric. Work a stitch, then take the thread across the back of the stitching area and work a back stitch on the opposite side. Repeat as required. When working around curves, use smaller stitches on the inside of the curve and slightly larger stitches on the outside of the curve to keep the stitches even.

Front of work   *Back of work*

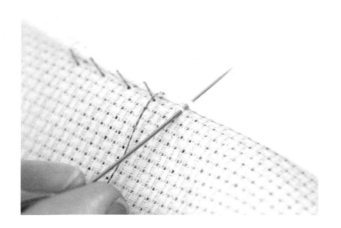

slip stitch

Slip stitch is usually used for hemming or joining two pieces of fabric. It is sometimes called invisible hemming, because only the tiniest of stitches are visible on the right side of the fabric. Use sewing thread and a fine needle, and begin with a knot hidden under the hem of the fabric. Bring the needle through the fold of the hem, then take it along the hem for a short distance. Pick up a few threads from the main part of the fabric and pass the needle through the fold of the hem. Pull the stitch through, then take another stitch in the same way. Continue stitching until the hem is complete.

stem stitch

Begin with a knot on the wrong side of the fabric. Bring the needle to the front and work a short stitch (1/8in or 4mm long, for example). Bring the needle up halfway along the stitch. (Hold the loop of thread out of the way as you stitch.) Pull the thread through, then work another stitch the same length as the first, this time bringing the needle up at the end of the first stitch. Continue in the same manner until the line of stitching is complete.

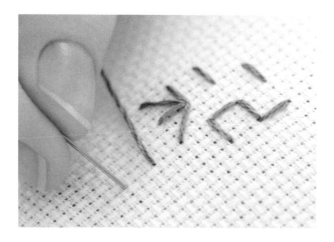

straight stitch

Straight stitches may be of any length. Starting with a knot on the wrong side of the fabric, work a single stitch with a crewel needle and embroidery thread in the direction given on the pattern. Straight stitches can be combined to produce stars, squares and many other angular shapes.

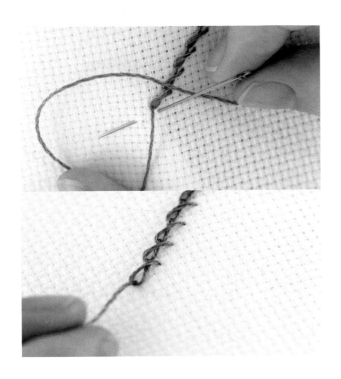

twisted chain stitch

Twisted chain stitch is a more decorative variation of chain stitch. Starting with a knot on the wrong side of the fabric, bring the needle and thread to the surface of the fabric at the start of the line to be embroidered. Carry the thread around in front of the needle in a large loop. Instead of inserting the needle into the same place as the thread comes up, cross it over and insert it a short distance to the right of the chain. Bring the needle back to the surface one stitch length away. Make sure that it is inside the loop of thread.

Pull the needle through the fabric. The loop should retain a rounded shape, but not be too loose. Work the next stitch in the same manner. You could also work twisted chain stitch as a single, detached stitch for a lazy daisy variation.

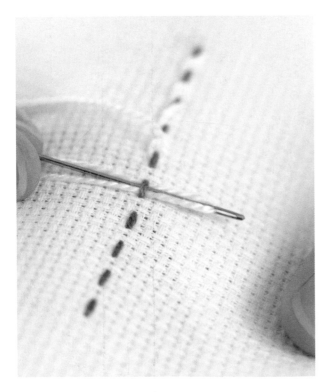

whipped running stitch

Whipped stitches are ordinary embroidery stitches that have a second thread twisted over them on the surface of the fabric. Running stitch is most commonly whipped, but back stitch, stem stitch and even chain stitch can also be whipped. The whipping thread is usually a different color than the thread used for the stitching.

Work the running stitch as described on page 135. Starting with a knot on the wrong side of the fabric and using a tapestry needle, bring the whipping thread to the surface through the same hole as the first running stitch. Pass the needle and thread under the first stitch from left to right, then under the second stitch from left to right.

If you are using a sharp needle, pass the eye end of the needle under the running stitch as shown in the photograph. This prevents the point of the needle from accidentally splitting the thread of the running stitch as it passes through.

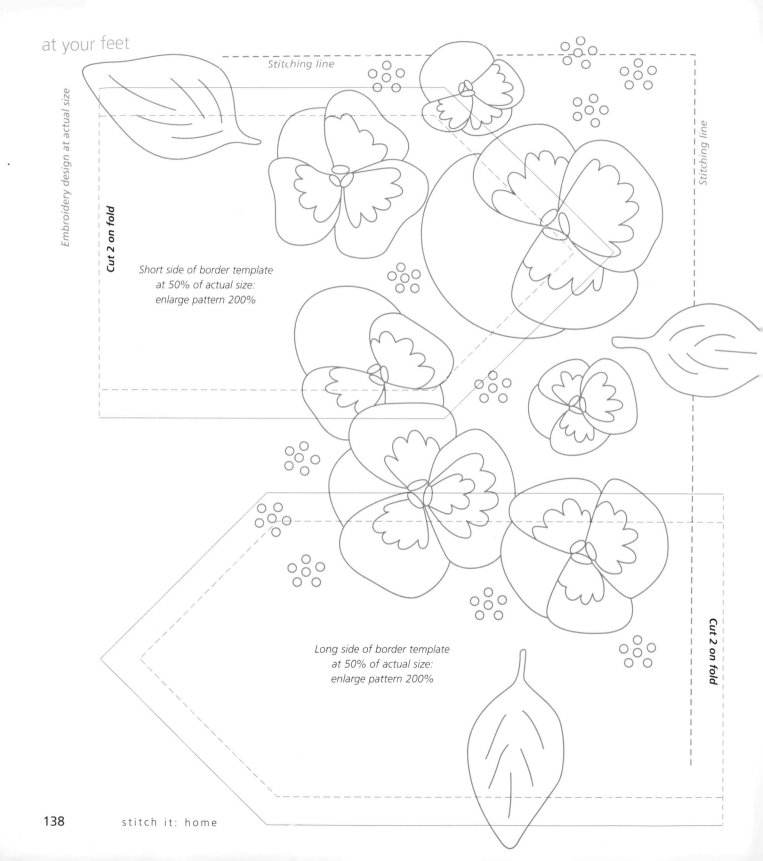

Stitching line

Stitching line

Stitching line

Embroidery design at actual size

Cut 2 on fold

Short side of border template
at 50% of actual size:
enlarge pattern 200%

Long side of border template
at 50% of actual size:
enlarge pattern 200%

Cut 2 on fold

DMC colour
☐ 3865
▨ 159
▨ 160
▧ 161
⌐ 823

Journal cover placement guide

Soft touch templates
at actual size

Ornament templates
at actual size

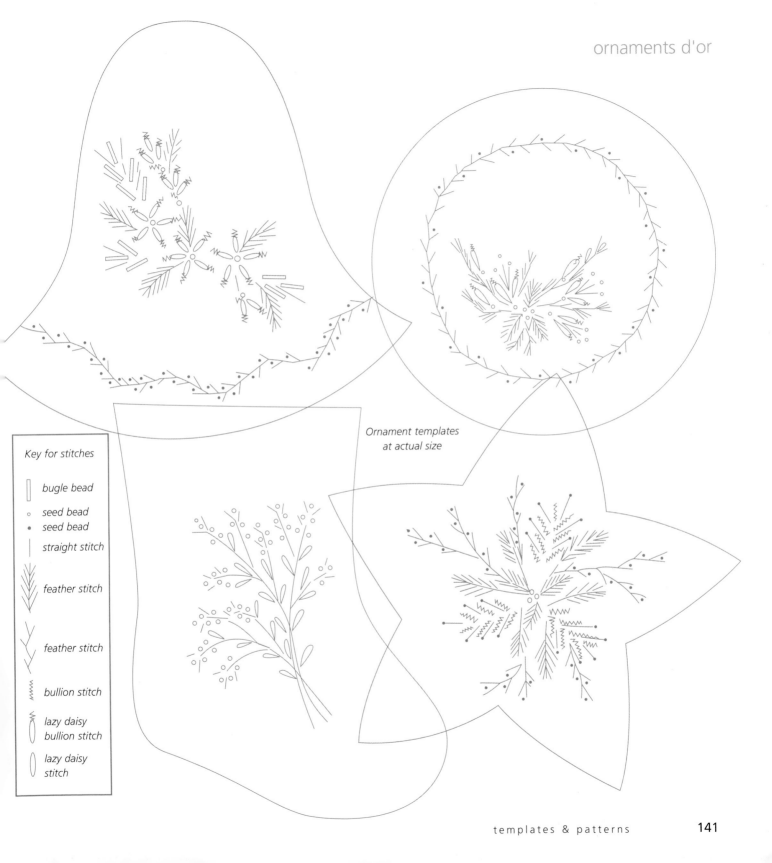

Ornament templates
at actual size

Key for stitches

	bugle bead
o	seed bead
•	seed bead
	straight stitch
	feather stitch
	feather stitch
	bullion stitch
	lazy daisy bullion stitch
	lazy daisy stitch

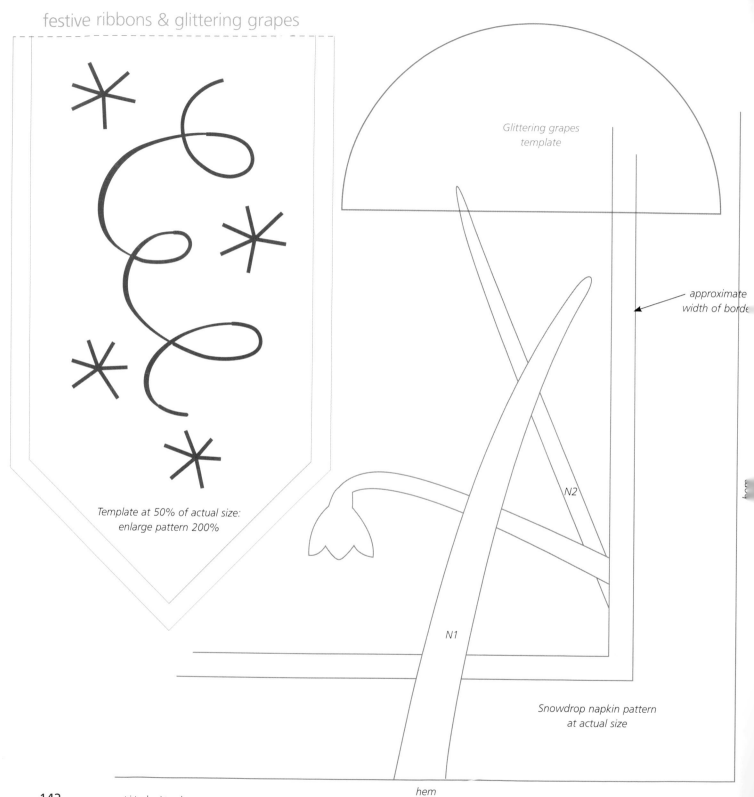

*Template at 50% of actual size:
enlarge pattern 200%*

*Glittering grapes
template*

*approximate
width of borde*

N2

N1

*Snowdrop napkin pattern
at actual size*

hem

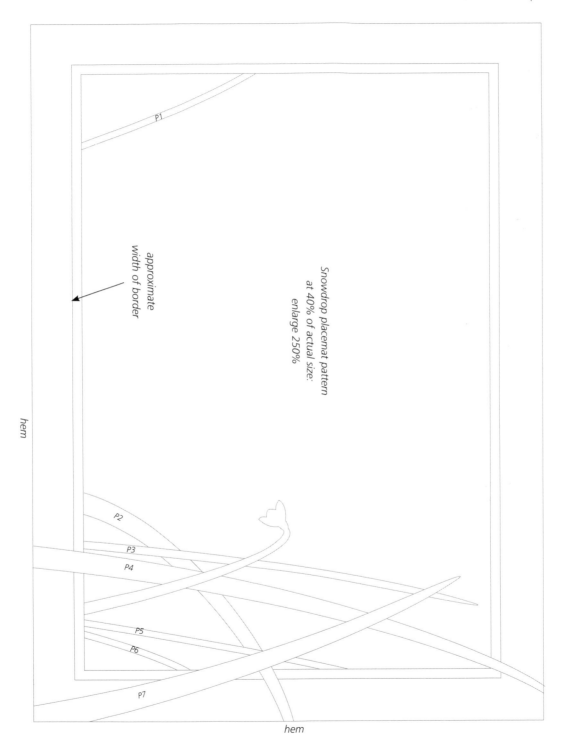

P1

approximate
width of border

*Snowdrop placemat pattern
at 40% of actual size:
enlarge 250%*

hem

P2

P3

P4

P5

P6

P7

hem

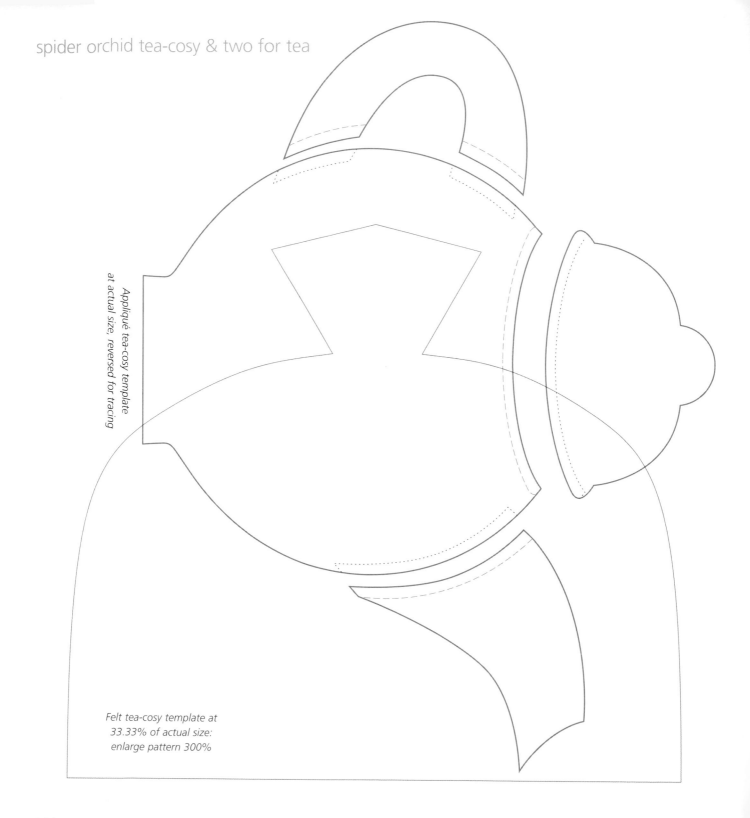

Appliqué tea-cosy template at actual size, reversed for tracing

Felt tea-cosy template at 33.33% of actual size: enlarge pattern 300%

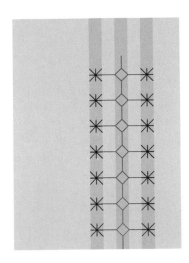

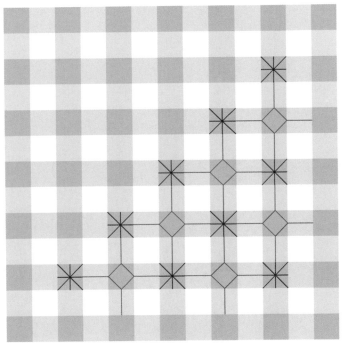

Placement guides

Good coffee is like friendship: rich and warm and strong. PAN AMERICAN COFFEE BUREAU

When one has tea and wine one will have many friends. CHINESE PROVERB

Bread is the warmest, kindest of words. Write it always with a capital letter, like your own name. RUSSIAN PROVERB

Love and scandal are the best sweeteners of tea. HENRY FIELDING

When one is hungry, everything is as sweet as honey. CHINESE PROVERB

Tea! Thou soft, thou sober, sage and venerable liquid. COLLEY CIBBER

The morning cup of coffee has an exhiliration about it which the cheering influence of the afternoon cup of tea cannot be expected to reproduce. OLIVER WENDELL HOLMES

Tea to the English is really a picnic indoors. ALICE WALKER

Suggested quotations: stitch according to graph on page 146

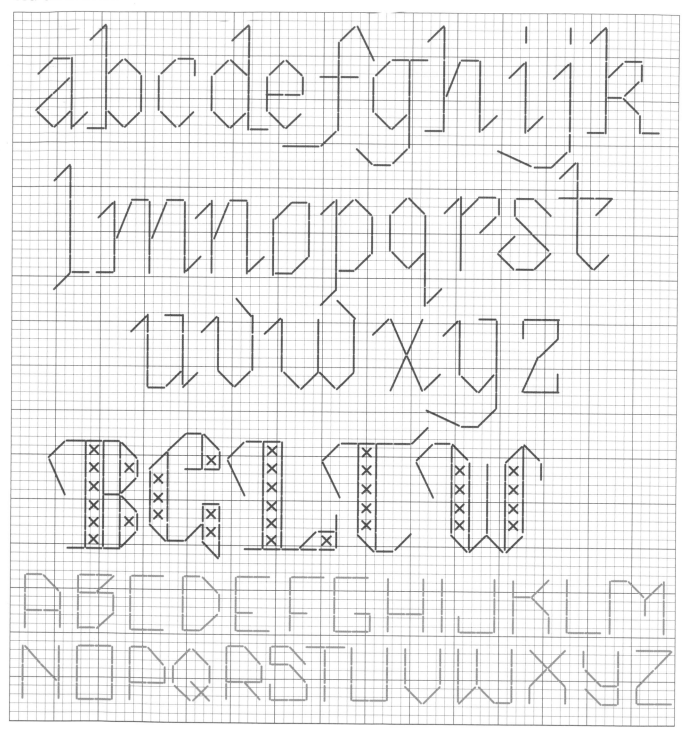

stitch it: home

abcdefg
hijklmn
pqrstuvw
xyz

2in (5cm)

*Monogram template at
80% of actual size:
enlarge pattern 125%*

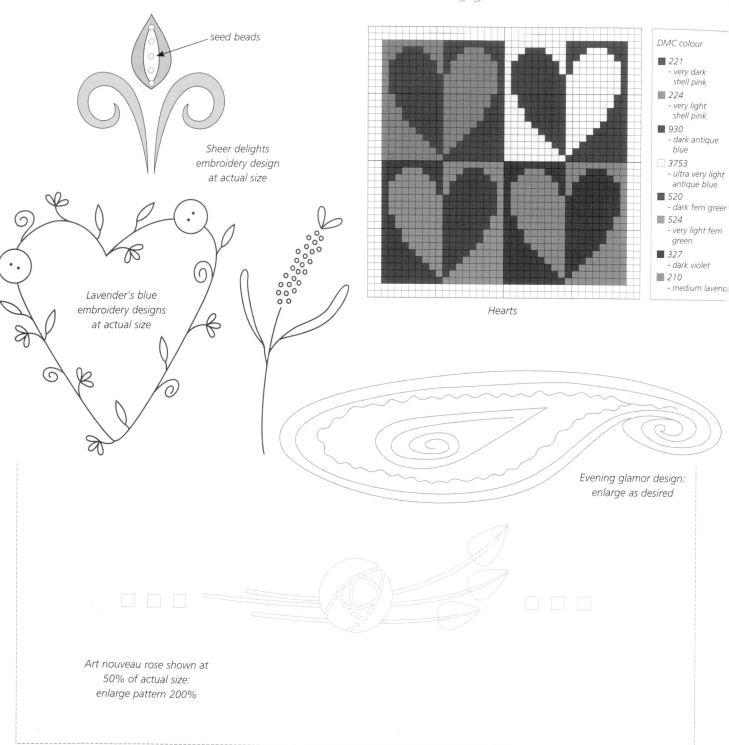

seed beads

Sheer delights
embroidery design
at actual size

Lavender's blue
embroidery designs
at actual size

DMC colour

■ 221
 - very dark
 shell pink

■ 224
 - very light
 shell pink

■ 930
 - dark antique
 blue

□ 3753
 - ultra very light
 antique blue

■ 520
 - dark fern green

■ 524
 - very light fern
 green

■ 327
 - dark violet

■ 210
 - medium lavenc

Hearts

Evening glamor design:
enlarge as desired

Art nouveau rose shown at
50% of actual size:
enlarge pattern 200%

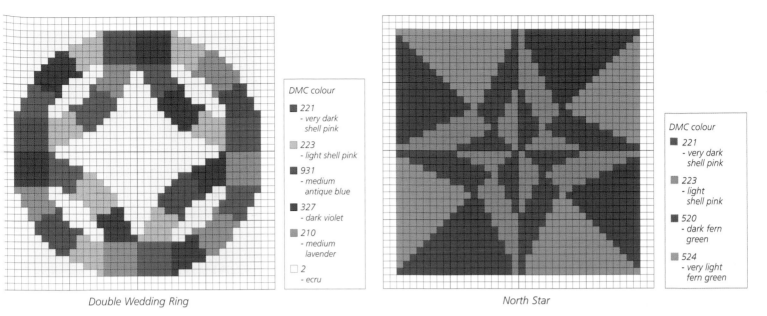

DMC colour

■ 221
- very dark
shell pink

■ 223
- light shell pink

■ 931
- medium
antique blue

■ 327
- dark violet

■ 210
- medium
lavender

□ 2
- ecru

Double Wedding Ring

DMC colour

■ 221
- very dark
shell pink

■ 223
- light
shell pink

■ 520
- dark fern
green

■ 524
- very light
fern green

North Star

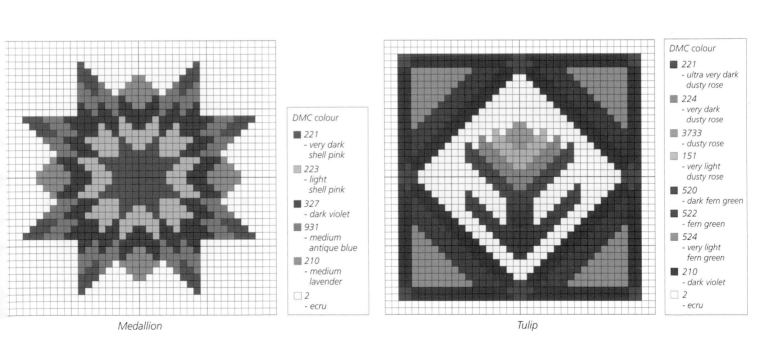

DMC colour

■ 221
- very dark
shell pink

■ 223
- light
shell pink

■ 327
- dark violet

■ 931
- medium
antique blue

■ 210
- medium
lavender

□ 2
- ecru

Medallion

DMC colour

■ 221
- ultra very dark
dusty rose

■ 224
- very dark
dusty rose

■ 3733
- dusty rose

■ 151
- very light
dusty rose

■ 520
- dark fern green

■ 522
- fern green

■ 524
- very light
fern green

■ 210
- dark violet

□ 2
- ecru

Tulip

index

index of artisans

acknowledgements

Thank you to the following people for their assistance with this book:

Heather and John Benbow

Humble Beginnings, Randwick, NSW

Meredith Kirton and Michael Bradford

Bronwyn Lear

Carla Mann

Lara Schilling

Maxwell Whybro

inspirations books

Editor
Melody Lord

Design and layout
Susan Cadzow, Red Pepper Graphics

Photography and styling
Sue Stubbs

Publisher
Margie Bauer

Country Bumpkin Publications
315 Unley Road, Malvern
South Australia 5061
Phone: 08 8372 7600
Fax: 08 8372 7601
Email: marketing@countrybumpkin.com.au
Website: www.countrybumpkin.com.au

Published in Australia by Inspirations books
Printed and bound in the U.S.A.

Stitch it: Home
ISBN 978 09804359 0 0